WHEN GOOD-BYE IS FOREVER

Learning to Live Again
After the Loss of a Child

John Bramblett

BALLANTINE BOOKS • NEW YORK

To hope.

Contents

Foreword

When my wife and I sustained the bone-crushing grief that accompanied the loss of our twenty-year-old son David, who was killed in a mountain climbing accident in New Hampshire, we found that there is a bond that quickly develops among those who have lost a child. John Bramblett and I met in the course of our professional pursuits and found we had two bonds: our Christian faith and the loss of a child. This book is about the reaction of a father to the death of his child, and the message is for any who face a difficult trial.

When John sent me the manuscript for this book and asked me to consider writing a preface, I was the Surgeon General of the United States. The ethics associated with that position prevented me from writing such a preface or endorsing a publication. Now that I have left government service, I am delighted to serve John and his family by introducing this book to you.

The description of the first hours after the death of Christopher Bramblett are especially sensitive. With John, you live through the agony—the agony of a parent who has lost a child suddenly and unexpectedly. That episode will never be erased from the lives of the immediate family, but it is assuaged by the understanding and sympathy of friends and acquaintances. However, when life goes on for others, the family inevitably feels that support has been withdrawn. John describes this feeling exceptionally well.

I have read many books about the loss of a child—you do that when you have lived through it—and there is always a new wrinkle that comes to light from another's experience. For example, John felt that he should not return to work too soon if he wished to function without anger and resentment. I can well understand that sense of frustration (although I never felt anger or resentment) because the problems of everyday life seem so trivial compared to the loss of your child. I chose the opposite solution: I plunged back into work immediately, even though my work at the time was dealing, in part, with parents who were in the process of losing their child through illness.

How true that we are all changed by the death of a child! John makes an excellent point that, although spiritual growth brings healing and peace, the pain of separation nevertheless remains.

The in-depth description of the days, weeks, and months that followed Christopher's death should be extremely helpful and encouraging to a bereaved parent, who usually wonders if his or her reaction or timetable of recovery is "normal." And the casual reader who did not have to face such a loss will find this section heart-rending.

John Bramblett concludes that parents who accept the death of their child as part of God's plan for their lives can eventually achieve a unique peace others cannot find. My wife and I concur.

C. Everett Koop

Acknowledgments

Many people have played an important role in the development of this book. My friends Susan Clark, Jim and Laurie Mandy, and Dennis and Mary Lou Lunderville read the original manuscript and provided invaluable input for later revisions.

At Ballantine, I am forever indebted to Toni Simmons and Robert Wyatt for acquisition of the book and for initial editorial support. Without the sensitivity of Caroline Cullen, who first read the manuscript and recommended it to Toni, publication would not have become a reality. Julie Garriot's wonderful queries and line editing are much appreciated. Finally my special thanks to Elizabeth Zack for her gracious acceptance of the role of final editor and for her hard work in seeing the book through the concluding stages of publication.

Preface

In the early spring of 1985 I encountered a wave of personal tragedy so overwhelming that I doubted I would survive its onslaught. First, I was diagnosed with a deadly form of cancer. The cancer diagnosis pushed me far down into the abyss of self-pity, and I began to distance myself from my family and those around me. The days immediately following the diagnosis seemed the darkest of my life. I felt I had hit rock bottom. Surely I could go no lower.

Then on April 17 of that same year—just three weeks after my cancer was discovered—I learned that desolation can come in degrees, and I had yet to reach its darkest depths. On that day my two-year-old son Christopher was killed as my wife watched helplessly nearby. In that instant I moved from my bed of self-pity to my dead son's side. As I knelt by Christopher, looking into the face of death, I began to take another look at life and at how poorly I was using whatever time I might have left.

As part of my reassessment, I decided to write a book about my family's experience in an attempt to help others facing similar tragedies. Although I am writing specifically for parents who have lost children, I am really writing for all of us who experience hurt in life. Pain and hurt are not exclusive; they eventually impact on all of our lives. Despite the unique circumstances that may surround our individual suffering, common threads of pain—of misery—bind together all of us who suffer. We can become aware of that bond if we are open enough to share our pain rather than trying to hide it. And if we share, sooner or later we find our burden lightened. There lies a truth—and if we seek it, some comfort—at the heart of the ironic adage: "Misery loves company."

Throughout life we experience an incredible number of things that hurt us; some we bring directly upon ourselves, while others seem beyond our control. Divorce hurts; physical and emotional abuse hurt; hunger hurts; death hurts. Hurt evokes a wide range of human emotions, yet its manifestations are remarkably similar. And while, in most cases, the intensity of our emotional response to the hurt is proportional to the enormity of the event that brought it on—a broken friendship is usually less devastating than a divorce, the loss of a job less crushing than the death of a child—our similarities, in the way we feel about and respond to these events, remain.

If you are not among the suffering when you read this account of my experience, I hope it will help you to reach out to those who are. Perhaps you are a friend who wonders what you can do to help. If so, you'll find suggestions for providing support throughout this book. If you are in pain, I hope it will help you put that pain in perspective and deal with it in a positive way.

The story I tell is about the death of my son and how his short life changed—and continues to change—the life of every member of my family, as well as the lives of those around us. The overall change has been remarkably positive, considering the intensity of the tragedy. If asked to choose between giving up all the growth that has come to us through this experience— the many ways we have changed for the better—and having Christopher with us again, of course we would immediately and joyfully welcome him back. Unfortunately, death does not allow us that choice.

But we as parents do have some choices available to us as we try to move beyond the devastation lying in the wake of the death of our child. The catch is that they will not be made without pain. We will face these choices about how to deal with our irreversible loss until we, too, leave this life. Through this account I hope to share with you some of the ways my family and I have dealt with Christopher's death, and the choices we have made and continue to make on a daily basis. If you have lost a child, you will no doubt find much common ground in our experiences.

Therefore, join me as we move through the weeks just preceding the diagnosis of my cancer and on toward that chill April day when I found myself kneeling by the body of my dead son. In the early chapters allow me to introduce you to my family, to our hopes and our dreams. Then walk with us as we encounter the shattering events that change our lives forever. Be at our sides in the first minutes, the first hours and days as we mourn and try to integrate the idea of our loss into our lives. Stand with us at Christopher's grave as we attempt to comprehend the totality of the coming separation. Listen as my wife and my children open their hearts to you. Consider with us the unfinished outcomes—the "if only's." Then learn how to fight the anger, the guilt, the frustration you feel. Learn how community, friends, and reaching out to others can ease the tremendous pain, and speeds up the longed-for healing. Finally, question with us the issues of faith, of a loving God. Share in our resolution of those difficult questions, but, more importantly, share with us in our hope.

While your journey may be very different from ours, may it also be made a little easier as we open our lives to you.

Life is difficult.
SCOTT PECK, M.D., *The Road Less Travelled*

CHAPTER 1

Our Last Child

IN 1978 MY family and I made a mutual decision to leave the suburban sprawl of the Washington, D.C. area and "retreat" to rural Vermont. We considered our upcoming move a retreat since we had lived briefly in Vermont once before, just prior to a job-related move to Washington in 1975. After three years in our nation's capital, we were burned out. We found Washington an appealing city with its rich history and cultural opportunities, but the pace and the growing congestion were more than we wanted to bear. We even coined a word that described our most frequent complaint about the area. Our home was in Fairfax County, Virginia. Almost invariably when we went out to eat or to see a movie, we would arrive to find a long waiting line or a sold-out event. One Saturday we tried to go bowling, play tennis, see a movie, and eat at a nearby family seafood house—all without success because of crowds of other Fairfaxians who were trying to do the same thing. After several unproductive hours in a hot car, we came home and coined our word: "Fairfaxed." We had been "Fairfaxed" all day. Still, we were able to manage a smile, knowing we would soon trade this unpleasant condition for the rural, green hills of Vermont.

1

Our memories of Vermont beckoned strongly enough that I had decided to take a substantial cut in pay to make the move. With my pregnant wife, Mairi, and our two children—John age ten, and Brian age seven—I moved to a tiny village in north-central Vermont. We were fortunate to find an old Victorian house on a quiet road at the edge of the village. There was a sizable river for fishing just a quarter-mile from our front door, and in the front yard was a two-hundred-year-old maple that we tapped for sap to make maple syrup in the spring. This was living. No getting "Fairfaxed" here.

On June 20, 1979, less than eight months after our return to Vermont, I was called from a meeting of the local Rotary club to take Mairi to the hospital for the delivery of what would be our first daughter. The meeting was being held at the Mount Mansfield Trout Club, an ancient frame building situated on a cold, clear lake tucked tightly against the downslope of Mount Mansfield—Vermont's highest mountain. The road was not especially cooperative as I raced for home to meet Mairi and drive her to the Medical Center Hospital in Burlington. Where the problem in Virginia would have been traffic, the difficulty here was the sharp S-turns and loose gravel. But we made the delivery room with time to spare, and within a week Mairi and our new daughter, Meghan, joined John, Brian, and me at home.

The next few years moved by in short flashes of summer green and long days of winter white. Over the course of those three years in Vermont, we invested heavily in upgrading our hundred–year–old home. Things like insulation (there was none!), replacing the coal cookstove in the kitchen, and cementing over the dirt floor of the cellar, to get rid of the musty smell that was still there from the flood of 1927, took up much of our time. We were beginning to realize that we weren't really cut out for the rigors or the costs of renovation. With a mix of emotions, we decided to sell our house and build on a piece of land we had recently purchased in the hills just outside our village. We had relocated more than twelve times in the past ten years because of my career. This home, we knew, would be our last.

At about the same time we decided to build a new home, we learned Mairi was pregnant again. And so we made another decision, with conviction: this would be our last baby. It was not an easy decision, but as we were now in our mid–thirties, we believed it was a good time to shift our focus from child-bearing to better raising and enjoying our family.

Mairi's delivery was to be a cesarean section, so when she entered the hospital, some of the mystery normally surrounding a birth was missing. Unlike many expecting parents, we knew the exact day and time our son would be born. Yes, some preliminary testing had provided us with the information that the baby would be a boy.

On December 17 Mairi was wheeled to the delivery room. As we had arranged with the doctor, I accompanied her, along with a camera for pictures of the birth of our last child. I had followed the doctor's instructions: eat a big breakfast and concentrate on the birth, not the surgical procedure. As he had predicted, I quickly became enthralled by the actual event of the birth. In my excitement I altogether escaped the queasiness I had expected to feel in watching the procedure. Standing at the head of the delivery table, I talked quietly with Mairi as the doctors—and Mairi—continued their work.

I suppose that the most amazing part of the surgical delivery was how quickly our son was born. In what seemed like less than five minutes after the surgery began, I saw his head emerging from the incision in Mairi's belly. My initial joy quickly turned to alarm when I saw that the baby's umbilical cord was wrapped in a tight circle around his head. Urgently the doctors tried to work the slippery cord free from its life-threatening grip. To my relief the rubbery cord finally came free, and the doctors lifted our little boy from my wife's abdomen. Leaving the security of the womb, Christopher (as we named him) threw back his hands as if he felt he was falling or perhaps to protest this glaring new world of light and noise. Those hands reaching into the air were really the first feature of Christopher's I noticed—they were large, larger than the hands of any of our previous children, and as my mind drifted ahead through the years, I saw them throwing baseballs and footballs with older brothers and with me on some day still far away.

As I studied Christopher's overall appearance, his umbilical cord once again drew the attention of the medical staff. A discussion between the doctors and nurses had ensued about the length of the cord. It was extremely long—in fact, the longest the doctors could ever recall having seen (over five feet in length!). There was a light moment as we all laughed about our new entry into the *Guinness Book of World Records*, and then the doctors began the time-consuming work of closing the cesarean as Christopher was wheeled off to the nursery in his Plexiglas isolette. Mairi and I had completed another cycle of birth—the fifth and our last. And while we had accepted this fact long before we entered the delivery room, it still struck a poignant chord as Mairi and I both quietly realized that this was the last time we would share the special moment of birth.

For a fleeting moment, my thoughts moved back to 1976, when, in this same hospital, Mairi had delivered another baby. I was absent from that delivery—not by choice but by circumstance. Mairi had been hospitalized for "the duration of the pregnancy" in March of that year due to a condition known as placenta privea. While taking a shower in her hospital room, the placenta had torn loose from the wall of the uterus, and she began hemorrhaging internally. She was rushed to the delivery suite for an emergency cesarean while a nurse called me at my office forty miles away. I raced to the hospital, arriving only in time to see Mairi briefly before the surgery began.

The baby, four months premature, weighed only thirty-one ounces and was just under eleven inches long. We named him Matthew Aidan (he and Christopher shared the same middle name), and we watched him struggle for four long weeks. Despite the excellent treatment he received, he died quietly in Mairi's arms one early spring morning in May after a particularly agonizing night of seizures.

But this birth was different. Mairi and our new baby were both healthy and we were able to bring our little boy—

Christopher Aidan—home just before Christmas in a tiny red Christmas stocking provided by the nurses who worked on the maternity ward. It was the first time he shared Christmas with us, and I think each of us appreciated what a very special gift he was.

But as we moved into the new year, life became difficult for Christopher. He weighed less at his six-week checkup than he did when he was born, and his respiratory system was constantly aggravated by the smoke that leaked from the woodstove in the parlor as we struggled to keep our old house marginally warm through the Vermont winter.

I found myself exceptionally tired in those first few months after Christopher's birth, worrying constantly about his sagging weight and his thick, mucousy cough. My exhaustion created tension between Mairi and me; I even began to question the soundness of the decision we had made to have this last baby. I began wondering whether we had, perhaps, lost our parenting skills in the three-and-a-half-year span between Meghan's birth and Christopher's.

As the cold, dark winter months wore on, my energy continued to diminish, and the tension between Mairi and me increased. But somehow we made it through that trying time, and, with love and an extra late-night bottle or two, Christopher survived his first Vermont winter. The days began to lengthen and warm, the snow disappeared, and our family turned the corner into spring and summer.

In August, with our little boy eight months old, we started the new house for which we had planned so long. Unfortunately the burden this created seemed to take up where the difficult winter had left off. My energy continued to diminish as we tried to manage the subcontracting ourselves in an effort to keep the building costs down. Mairi and I spent hours staining clapboard, painting trim, and stuffing insulation. The boys and Meghan also helped when we had a job they could handle. Our schedule seemed to be controlled not by us but by the new house. On a typical night in late August John and I worked until midnight tarring the foundation of the house, our only light coming from the headlights of our old Jeep. The work was endless; the summer came and went by quickly without its usual rejuvenating moments of leisure.

Adding to the strain caused by the new house was the stress I experienced in other areas of my life. I was selected for a supervisory position at work and was having difficulty with an employee who was suffering from Post-Vietnam Stress Syndrome. I was also serving on the village's board of zoning adjustment and as a director in the local Rotary Club. The demands on my life were becoming increasingly difficult; they piled precariously one on top of another like a house of cards. My ability to cope with the accumulating stress was near its limit

In October, I came home from a meeting late one night and was greeted at the door by the distressed faces of my wife's parents who were visiting from Ohio. Christopher had suddenly become very sick and was having serious breathing difficulties. They were preparing to leave for the hospital emergency room just as I arrived. Running upstairs, I found Mairi in our bedroom holding our nine–month–old son close to a vaporizer that threw out steaming clouds of hot vapor into the chill air.

When I saw Christopher's face I knew how serious the situation was. He was gasping for air, and with each sucking breath, his thin chest collapsed. Mairi wrapped Christopher in a blanket while I started the car, and we rushed thirty miles through the dark October night to the Medical Center Hospital in Burlington.

As we drove along the winding interstate, I silently questioned how much longer I could continue under all of this stress. My first concern was for Christopher, but I also realized I, too, had little left to give in the face of a seemingly endless onslaught of struggles.

The emergency-room doctor's diagnosis was viral croup. Christopher was admitted to the pediatric ward and placed in an oxygen tent. The moment he was laid down, he panicked at this plastic-bubble barrier between him and the world outside—and his panic only escalated his breathing problems. As Mairi and I stood beside the tent looking in at our little boy, now so fragile, so frightened, I sensed how very much alone he must have felt.

My needs as a father far outweighed conformance with hospital policy; I lifted the side of the vinyl tent, managing to squeeze my upper body in with Christopher, holding him close to me in an effort to calm him. His tiny body was hot with fever and shaking with fear. As I held him in the darkened room, I knew I could not leave him. I would stay with him for the duration of this illness—regardless of how long it might last. Mairi reluctantly kissed us good-bye and returned home to care for the rest of the family.

An orderly brought a cot into the room for me, and Christopher and I spent the first of three restless long nights as the night nurses made frequent rounds to check on their young patients. More than once I woke to the glare of a flashlight and the sound of footsteps moving in the direction of Christopher's oxygen tent. I would lie there in the darkened room, listening to the sounds of the nurse checking Christopher, drifting off to sleep only as the soft patter of her steps faded into the darkness of the silent corridor.

As the days in the hospital slowly passed, Christopher grew more comfortable with his new surroundings. I also think he realized that I was not going to leave him alone. During those three days, my busy world was put on hold. It was a sort of awakening for me, for it was during this unexpected hospitalization that I faced something I had consciously blocked from my mind since 1976—the death at the age of four weeks of our premature son Matthew in this same hospital. Once again I was directly confronted with the realization of just how vulnerable our children are. Never had there been problems like this with our other children. My attachment to Christopher grew as I became fully aware of just how fragile he was.

Christopher continued to have respiratory problems, but he managed to fight his way through this occurrence as well as a similar episode the following April. Although the source of these problems could not be pinned down, I am convinced in retrospect that our woodstove and its invisible leaks were the primary cause of irritation to his sensitive lungs.

In March of 1984 we moved into our new house. Much to our joy, Christopher's health began to improve almost immediately. He took to the new environment of level floors and open space with the excitement of a new puppy just let off the leash. The old house had been an obstacle course of multiple staircases and uneven, wide-board floors, but this new house was a toddler's paradise. The first floor was virtually obstruction-free, and Christopher's mobility skills quickly sharpened. The months following our March move sped past us as we continued to finish much of the work on our new home.

In early October Mairi and I shared a day with Christopher that has become priceless. The leaves on the Vermont maples were near their peak color, we had already had several frosts and a dusting of snow, and we assumed we had seen the last of summer's warmth. One Sunday, however, we awoke to beautiful sunshine pouring in our bedroom window. It was, as I recall, the last "Indian summer" day that year. We quickly dressed and went outside to bask in the early-morning sunshine.

As the morning grew into afternoon, the light on the blazing reds and yellows of the maple trees scattered about our woods and the nearby mountains were as beautiful as we had ever seen. The day seemed almost enchanted. Christopher and Meghan spent most of the afternoon outside in the yard with us. Sometime in the late afternoon Mairi suggested that I photograph Christopher. As our family had grown, we seemed to have less time and took fewer and fewer pictures of the children. Each of them was so special to us, but we seemed to take their presence for granted, and pictures simply didn't get taken.

I found my camera and, taking Christopher's tiny hand, walked with him out through the old overgrown pasture that was now our side yard. Along the way we stopped and picked some stalks of milkweed, the downy pods exploding their whiteness into the gentle breeze and warm afternoon sunshine. When we reached the old stone wall bordering our property, I found a spot under the maples to photograph Christopher. Lifting him, I placed him gently on a smooth rock at the top of the old stone wall. As I took each photograph, I kept thinking how special these moments were. The contrast in colors—the gray stone wall, the frosted yellow ferns, the iridescent leaves of the maples, Christopher's white-blond hair—all seemed to harmonize with the rest of the magic offered by this unique fall day.

Christopher cooperated beautifully while I photographed him. He seemed preoccupied with something far in the distance, holding his milkweed stalk tightly in one hand while he stared out in the general direction of the line of mountains to the west of our home. With each movement of his hand, milkweed spilled into the air and floated softly to the leaf-covered ground at the base of the stone wall.

When Christopher and I returned to the house, we met Mairi in the yard. I told her about the picture session at the stone wall, and my exact words to her were, "I know that someday these pictures will be very special to us." Little did I know how true my statement would turn out to be.

The leaves were soon gone; November came and went. We had our usual bouts with the cold wet days and chilling winds of that month, and December was once again on us all too quickly. Despite the deepening winter, the entire family looked forward to the upcoming holiday season.

This particular Christmas, Christopher's third, was very special. He had grown into a beautiful, towheaded little boy with a pleasant disposition and physical abilities well beyond his age. He could throw his small toy football like a pro, was on ice skates before his second birthday, and even owned a small hockey stick, which he used in imaginary games with his older brother John, who was now playing high school hockey.

When we put up our Christmas tree that year, Christopher immediately assumed the role of inspector general, carefully reviewing every ornament from the lowest branches up to those at the top of his limited reach. In particular he was drawn to the tiny wooden mice that rode in little cars and hung from small trapezes—all apparently calling to him, "Take me!" And

Christopher, not wanting to disappoint those cheery little fellows, obliged. More than once we found him sitting quietly in a corner of the living room, turning a mouse ornament over and over in his hands, studying it as though it were a living thing. His blue eyes reflected his seriousness as he clutched his mouse, and when we asked him what he was doing, he would simply answer in a voice just above a whisper, "My mouse?" His statements were often two-word questions, especially as he wondered about ownership: Was this *his* mouse or someone else's? We explained to him that in this case it could be his mouse, but that it should be back on the tree with all of its friends.

Each time we put the mouse back Christopher would follow us, nestling very close to Mairi and me as the tree's twinkling blue, green, and red lights reflected in his eyes. Standing there in complete silence, he would stare at the wooden mice, the shining tinsel, and the tree itself, sometimes reaching out and gently touching the balsam needles or a strand of silvery tinsel. As he watched the tree vibrating from his touch, I saw the little boy of the past two years transforming before my eyes, moving into a stage of interactive awareness with the world around him and experiencing for the first time the awe, wonder, and magic of Christmas.

Looking back on that Christmas of 1984, I see it as a sort of "coming out" for Christopher. On Christmas morning he romped around in his yellow teddy-bear pajamas with their plastic-bottomed feet that seemed like ice skates on our shiny hardwood floors. He overdosed on his gifts and on the colorful cascade of wrapping paper that seemed to be everywhere. He literally trembled with excitement as he unwrapped the homemade "care bear" Mairi had gotten for him and the Matchbox cars that his older brother Brian "handed down" to him. Once in a while he took a spill on the floor as those slick pajama feet failed to keep up with his warp-speed rounds of the living room.

It almost seemed as though Christopher and Christmas had both "arrived" at the same time; and yet, despite the warm joy we shared in our new home on that cold December day, Mairi and I felt something of a fleeting melancholy as we watched our four children go through this beautiful ritual of Christmas. We remembered a time not so long ago, when John was in a pair of those same yellow pajamas . . . then Brian, then Meghan. In just a few short Christmases, I thought, Christopher, too, would trade in his pajamas for cutoffs, his Matchbox cars for some sort of Walkman. All too soon this little boy— our last—would grow up, leaving behind the innocence we saw in him this Christmas. I knew that some of the special Christmas magic that comes only from the innocence of little boys and girls would be packed away with those yellow pajamas.

The cold months after Christmas moved slowly for us, as they often do here in Vermont. Spells of snow and ice punctuated the days as did interludes of bitter cold followed by unusual thaws. When March arrived the entire family was anxious for the warm days and sun-filled skies of late spring; they were now at least within the realm of imagination.

On March 12 I had an office visit with my dermatologist as part of a follow-up program for a new drug being tested for FDA approval. The drug, Minoxidil, was being tested for its ability to grow hair. A balding friend and I had teased and cajoled each other into becoming participants in the study. Prior to the visit I had noticed a small, innocuous-looking mole on the front of my left leg just below the knee. I couldn't remember the mole being there for very long, and with some mild embarrassment at raising such a trivial issue, I asked the doctor to take a look at it.

To my surprise he reacted with noticeable concern, calling the mole "highly suspicious" and advising me that it should be taken off right away. Startled, I asked him what he meant by "right away." His face was grim as he advised me that it should be removed within the next week. My pulse quickened and my palms grew damp as we discussed the reason for the urgency—the possibility that the mole was malignant, that it could be a very deadly form of cancer called melanoma. I vividly remember the feeling I had as we moved our discussion further into the valley of fear that initially engulfs those who discover that they have, or may have, cancer.

Most of the next week was spent in what I can only describe as a sort of suspended animation. I was trying without much success to be optimistic and denying the possibility that I might have cancer. On Wednesday, March 20, I had surgery to remove the mole and some surrounding tissue. The pathology report, I was told, would be back possibly as early as two days later, on a Friday.

There was no report on Friday, and I spent a restless weekend waiting for Monday. At a party on Saturday night, I found it very difficult to partake as usual in the frivolity and small talk. My mind was locked on the surgery of the past Wednesday—and on the pending pathology report. When I called on Monday, there was still no report. Tuesday, no report. I began to panic as I teetered on the brink of the possibilities that faced me.

With each day that passed, I grew more nervous. Yet I knew that I owed no one any apologies for the anxiety I felt. Things became really awkward on Wednesday when I called once again from my office and spoke with the dermatology nurse. She seemed uncomfortable as she explained to me that, even if the results of my test were back, she could not give them to me; they would have to come directly from the doctor. The strain in her voice was evident, and as my mind processed the real message behind her words, the red flag went up.

As we talked, I repeated out loud the thought that was now screaming inside my head. "This doesn't sound good to me; there must be a problem." She told me that my doctor had been called down to pathology to review my slides, and she would have him call me when he returned to his office—within the hour.

Time passed slowly. Finally my doctor called. His voice was subdued, serious. I knew even before he told me that the tests were positive. I had cancer—a melanoma, a potentially deadly mole with invasive tendencies. We talked about the possibility of its spreading, of the limited types of treatment available, and of the need for more surgery—"major, more extensive surgery," the doctor said, involving a skin graft. And once again he emphasized the words "right away."

I left my office in a daze. As I drove the long stretch of interstate to my home, I tried to imagine breaking the news to the family. How could I explain to them something that still seemed so unreal to me?

On arriving home I came up with the pretense of having Mairi go to a neighbor's with me. Once we were in the car I told her the results of my pathology tests. She stared at me in disbelief as I explained the serious nature of the cancer and the need for more surgery. At first the silence in the car was broken only by the noises of the bumpy dirt road we were driving on; then there were sobs and soft shudders as we turned the car toward home and discussed how we would tell the children.

They handled the news better than Mairi and I. I was thankful for their youthful optimism. My son John chided me for using saccharin, though there was, of course, no relationship between it and my form of cancer. His touch of unintended humor relieved some of the stress we were all feeling. On April 2 I was back in the operating room once again.

I in the burying place see
Graves shorter there than I;
From death's arrest no age is free.
Young children too may die.
New England Primer 1688

CHAPTER 2

The Specter of Death

As I LAY on my back on the operating table for the second time in less than two weeks, the future that had seemed so secure—the one which I had taken for granted—was now seriously clouded by the sudden change in my health. The moments passed slowly as the surgeon made a substantial incision—almost six inches long and two inches wide—and removed all the tissue down to the muscle and bone of the shin of my left leg.

I remember the buzzing sound of the instrument he used to remove skin from my thigh for the graft; I remember looking down the length of my body at my leg, which at one point in the surgery was lifted up high in the air. There was no feeling, just the bizarre image of a leg that seemed to be floating in front of me—as if it didn't belong to my body. And yet I knew full well that it did.

To insure a positive graft I was kept virtually immobile in the hospital for six days. Easter came and passed in the small, dark hospital room, while at my home a group of friends and my wife hid eggs for the children in the early April sunshine. On April 8, the Monday following Easter, I was allowed to come home to recuperate.

Coming home I was faced with new problems of my own invention. My newly discovered cancer was immediate and threatening; this was enormously different from the day-to-day risks of living, which we casually accept and to which we are so accustomed. In the light of this new anxiety, my attitude toward my family changed dramatically. I wanted my wife's total sympathy, but while she was concerned for me, she was also, not unreasonably, concerned for herself and our family. My cancer threatened her framework of stability—stability we had built together in sixteen years of marriage. I quietly studied my children, especially the two youngest—Christopher and Meghan—and I pictured them without a father—quite specifically, without me. I found myself bitter. More than that, I was frightened.

Those first days at home, I stayed up late into the night facing the specter of death—not immediate death, really, but the agonizing death that slowly tears away at the body, coming at its own whim after intolerable suffering. Those late nights were responsible for a new habit of sleeping late in the mornings—an unhealthy escape from the fear and the lingering pain of the surgery. Excessive sleep—and the depression it so strongly suggests—became my way of dealing with the possibilities that faced me.

And I felt shocked by the hideous condition of my leg. The graft was raw, outlined with green-and-yellow pockets of pus. It bled through several bandages a day. Christopher would sometimes come up to me when I had taken the bandage off to clean the wound and stare for minutes at the ugly scar. Looking up into my eyes with deep concern, he would ask one of his famous two-word questions: "Daddy's ouch?"

Prior to my surgery I had prided myself on my physical condition. For over a year I had exercised regularly, lifting weights and running several miles each day to make myself "healthy." I felt I was beginning to recover from the stress of the past two years, just beginning to enjoy some of the things life "owed" me. Now I saw the emptiness of all my efforts as I faced months of recuperation from the operation. With each day that passed I found it more difficult to rise above my self-pity. Tension and irritability dominated my waking hours; fear and anxiety plagued my sleepless nights.

On April 16 I returned to my surgeon to have the stitches removed from my graft. Mairi, Christopher, and I drove the thirty miles to Burlington together, stopping on the way home to buy some clams to be steamed for lunch. Once at home I steamed the clams while Christopher watched. As usual, he asked for one to play with while I worked at the stove. He enjoyed touching the clam's extended spout, especially because the clam would squirt a little stream of water at Christopher as he withdrew his tiny finger. It had become a game—Christopher versus the clam. I'm not sure who won, but the squirting clam eventually ended up in the steamer along with its associates.

I melted some butter and sat down at the kitchen table, ready to begin a messy but delicious New England feast. Christopher joined me, asking for clams, one at a time. "My kwam?" he would ask as I stripped one of its shell and "sock," dipped it into the melted butter, and handed it to him.

A moment later he was choking on one of the clams. He gagged and immediately began to turn a dusky purple—but he managed to cough the clam out even before I could try to help him. I was shaken, as I was every time he had one of his choking episodes. Of all the calamities of childhood, choking frightened me the most. Looking at Christopher as he frowned at the dislodged clam, I told him, "Christopher, you will be the death of me yet!"

We spent the rest of the early spring day in the yard together. I lay on the chaise lounge, resting my leg. Christopher ran around the yard in the unusually warm sunshine. Once he ran toward the road, far from my reach, and I did all I could do in my disabled condition—I shouted at him to come back. He turned toward me, his tiny lips in a pout as he walked back down the driveway. When he reached me I explained that the cars in the road could hurt him, not knowing if he really understood the danger. A few minutes later, as we were tossing his small toy football, he suddenly stopped and turned to face the road once again. He had heard the noise of a large vehicle in the distance. As it drew closer and rounded the curve at our driveway, I saw it was the school bus.

Christopher grinned at me and announced the arrival with an excited "School bus!" I told him it was okay to run up the driveway now to meet his older brothers and sister. And as he did, I smiled, appreciating the special friendship among these four children spread so far apart in years.

Toward evening the weather changed dramatically. Storm clouds gathered on the distant horizon, piling up high above the ridges of the Green Mountains just to the west of our home. A little before dusk a vicious thunderstorm roared over our hill. Huge raindrops rattled against our windows, and the wind blew over the chaise and some other things I had left in the yard earlier in the afternoon. Within an hour the rain had changed to heavy wet snow, and it quickly coated the telephone and power lines—and the first spring flowers, which had opened earlier in the day. The wet snow weighted the lines, and the high winds tore at them. Soon we were without power. The afternoon had grown dark, and as I left for my first Rotary Club meeting since my surgery, Mairi was rounding up candles to light the rest of our evening.

I was greeted warmly that night by my fellow club members, and I sensed their genuine concern for me and my health. At one point in the meeting the president asked me if I wanted to say anything to the club. As I looked around me at a sea of somber faces—friends who knew how potentially serious my newly discovered cancer was—I took a deep breath and simply told them that I had learned just how quickly life can change, and that, despite my diagnosis, I was optimistic. I encouraged them to slow down, to enjoy life, to remember that there are no guarantees. My voice trembled as I spoke, for I was only beginning to absorb the truth of my own words.

After the meeting I asked a good friend if we could go

somewhere to talk for a little while; the gloom of the stormy evening had somehow permeated my mood, and I was suddenly very depressed. We stopped at the local Holiday Inn, and as we sat and talked, I told this dear friend that I felt as if my life was over. I was now facing cancer with a young family I might not live to raise. It all seemed so hopeless. My friend could do little more than listen and shake his head. He knew how legitimate my despair was, but there was nothing he could do except offer his support.

I returned home exhausted. The power was still out, and I was greeted by the flickering light of a solitary candle in our living room. In the fireplace were dying embers of a fire Mairi had built earlier in the evening, but she and the children were already in bed. I climbed the stairs and crawled into bed, once again dreading the day to come. Another day to struggle through, another day to deal with the uncertainty of my future.

And so on the morning of April 17, 1985, at 9:30, I found myself in a restless half-sleep while Christopher clamored outside my bedroom door. He wanted to come in, he wanted to see me. In my selfishness I lay there, hoping that Mairi would come and get him, and within a few minutes she did. They went downstairs, and I was relieved to hear Christopher playing cheerfully with some toy or, perhaps, an imaginary friend. John and Brian were at school; Meghan was still in her room.

Just before ten o'clock I pulled myself from bed, filled the tub, and climbed into the steaming water to soak the ugly, oozing skin graft. Meghan came in to say good morning—and as we talked, I suddenly heard unearthly screaming from somewhere outside our house. The screams were hysterical, as if someone were being attacked or beaten. They seemed to be coming from the general direction of our nearest neighbor's house some two hundred yards away, but when I listened more intently, I realized that the screams were much closer than they had seemed at first.

I felt torn—frozen with the fear of learning what the screams meant yet desperate to find out. Before I could move, Meghan asked me what was wrong. I could only tell her the truth: I didn't know. With my heart now pounding so hard I thought it might explode from my chest, I got out of the tub and went to the top of the stairs, grasping my towel about me as I ran.

Looking down, I saw that our front door was open. It was a cold, clear day, and the open door signalled that something was terribly wrong. It was then I realized the screams were Mairi's. I had never heard her like this before. My first thought was that she was being attacked. Suddenly she appeared in the open doorway, and before I could ask, she was on the downstairs phone.

"Please send the ambulance, Oh, God, please. . . ."

My voice broke as I called to her, asking what had happened. Her words exploded in my ears. "Christopher's dead! He's dead, John. Please do something. . . ."

With my mind swirling, I grabbed a pair of pants and ran to the bottom of the stairs. In the instant of time it took me to reach the front door, I denied the possibility that this could be happening. Yet looking out the open door, I saw my son in his little plaid snowsuit and his tiny white boots lying horribly still in our driveway. Ten or fifteen yards away, a large truck—a garbage truck—had pulled off into our yard. My thoughts struggled against the obvious connection. A wave of nausea rushed over me.

The garbage truck comes to pick up our trash only once a week, on Wednesdays, and then for no more than a few minutes. In that short span of time Christopher had made his way to the driveway—unseen by the driver—and been run down as the truck pulled away from our house.

Glancing quickly back up the stairs, I saw Meghan's face. She asked in a voice shaking with fear if Christopher really was dead. Telling her that I didn't know, I had no choice but to leave our trembling five-year-old alone as I ran to be with Christopher.

The surreal dream was crashing down on me again. First the cancer, now this. Dear God, could this be real?

I ran the twenty-five yards to where Christopher lay on his back in the driveway—at first afraid to look at his face. As I knelt over him, I knew immediately that he was dead. But in my denial and confusion, I took the time to carefully wipe some sand from his eyelid, wanting not to hurt him before I raised his eyelid to check his pupil. The pupil was fixed, his pulse was still, and although his hands were warm, the spirit that had animated his precious little body was gone.

There was nothing that could be done. In no more than an instant we had lost the child who had struggled more than any of our other children to survive in his two short years of life. In the intensity of this moment, with nowhere to hide, no way to make things better, I was confronted by the revelation of my selfishness and my own self-pity. Not more than thirty minutes earlier, I had denied him entry into my room while I wallowed in my weariness. Now he was gone. And in the utter stillness of that moment—alone with Christopher—I put my self-pity away for good.

Mairi came and knelt beside me, and we shared this last moment with Christopher, holding him close as we waited for the emergency officials to arrive. Once again we found ourselves holding a dying child, much as we had done under different circumstances in the loss of Matthew.

The unbearable pain, the unfathomable sorrow and emptiness that had followed Matthew's death surged over us again. As hard as Matthew's death was, however, its blow was softened by the fact that he was an infant who never came home, who never really knew us. He'd had no chance to develop a personality, and we had never had the chance to develop the deep attachment to him that can grow only with time.

But Christopher was all the things Matthew never had a chance to be. He talked with us, shared our lives, took our love and gave it back. He was our last child.

And now we held him for the final time, desperately hoping we would wake up from the terrible dream we seemed to be caught up in—the long-running, repulsive nightmare of death that had already filled our lives with so much despair over the past several weeks. But as the ambulance arrived with its siren wailing, we knew all too well this dream would not end; this dream was real.

O, in one hour what years of anguish crowd.
BULWER-LYTTON, *Richelieu*, Act iii, sc 1

CHAPTER 3

The First Hours

WHETHER WE HAVE had months to prepare for that final, inevitable moment as our child struggles through the throes of some fatal disease, or whether our child is snatched away in a single terrifying instant—as Christopher was—we cannot find words to convey the emptiness and pain that surge over us again and again in those first hours.

In the initial moments following Christopher's death, Mairi and I held him in the ambulance, pleading with the crew, asking for help where none was possible. In those very early moments we were forced to take the first step in the long process of accepting his death, the first step in letting him go.

Especially in the case of accidental death, we are faced with an onslaught of people who may be total strangers to us. Ambulance crews, police, emergency personnel, funeral directors, and others enter this sensitive time by necessity—not by invitation. While our emotions might have us withdraw from contact with these professionals, we have to realize that they play an essential role in meeting our immediate needs. Their duties must be carried out. Though their presence will often seem an intrusion, it is something we simply must accept.

21

And so we were surrounded by a mix of people we knew and didn't know—state and local police, our family doctor, and a few close friends who had learned quickly of the accident. Someone—I can't remember who—suggested that we go back into the house. It was time for the ambulance to take Christopher's body to the funeral home.

We found it so incredibly hard to give Christopher's body up. He was still warm. The warmth offered us false hope. He had never left us before, in any fashion, and yet now we were called on to let him go forever. As part of this process, we had to give him up to someone else for the first time—someone who would prepare his body for burial. And so while still in the grip of the shock following his death, we let go. This physical letting go would be followed by a deeper emotional letting go in the weeks and months that lay ahead.

Clutching each other as we returned to the house, Mairi and I were assaulted by a wild range of emotions and thoughts. Denial that our child was dead. Confusion as to exactly how the accident had happened. Panic as we tried to absorb the cruel reality that Christopher's life was now over. The beginnings of an emptiness that would only grow deeper as we realized our loss. We immediately went to Meghan, who was in the arms of a caring neighbor. We took her and, holding her close to us, tried to explain what had happened.

Meghan's first words to me were the same she had spoken when I left her at the top of the stairs: "Is Christopher dead?" I told her yes, he was. With the paradoxical mix of wisdom and innocence of the very young, she asked a second, more devastating question: "Does that mean he isn't going to live here anymore?" I could barely speak as I pulled her close to me and repeated her own words in a broken whisper. "Yes, Meghan, that means he isn't going to live here anymore." It was amazing that she had already begun to integrate the meaning of this tragedy into our family life.

At the time of the accident a state trooper had volunteered to go to the local high school to pick up John and Brian. When the patrol car returned, Mairi and I met our boys in the same driveway where less than an hour earlier their brother had been killed. They had already heard about the immensity of our loss. For a time we simply held each other and wept; few words were spoken. Finally the boys asked some questions about what had happened, but for the most part we shared our pain and grief in silence. Then, arm in arm, we walked back down the driveway to the house.

During those first few hours, Mairi and I wandered about the house in a daze. As we drifted aimlessly from room to room, one or both of us would burst into tears as we found some misplaced toy of Christopher's or saw some crayon mark on the wall that we had scolded him for just last week. I moved into the kitchen and broke down completely as I found a half-eaten apple at his place at our table—his tiny teeth marks were still visible on its shiny red skin.

Our emotions could not absorb the terrible fact of our loss. There were anguished moments when we would stare at each other in speechless disbelief followed by longer periods of stupor in which memories of the hours and days just before this nightmare began replayed themselves again and again. Although our minds tried to block out the tragedy, we were utterly helpless in our attempt to control our thoughts.

Within thirty minutes after the ambulance had left, we were forced to begin dealing with a series of seemingly impossible tasks—the most important of which was to break the word of Christopher's death to our parents. That was especially difficult for me, since I had not yet told my parents about my cancer. My plans had been to do so later in the summer, when we visited them in Atlanta. At that time, my healing would be more complete. There would be no way to hide the surgery from them now. My leg required continuous care, and I was walking with a limp; when my parents arrived for the funeral they would have to be told. So they would be jolted by two devastating revelations: first, the death of their grandson, then the life-threatening cancer of their own son. Despite their faith, which I knew was strong, I doubted their ability to cope with all of this at once.

The mobility of our modern world has, in so many cases, put thousands of miles between us and our families. As I thought about the horrible news I must now deliver over the telephone, I pictured my parents, twelve hundred miles away in Atlanta, and their reaction. I knew they must not be alone when they heard of Christopher's death. In what was perhaps my most rational moment since the accident itself, I called information and got the number of the office where my closest cousin, Mary Ann, worked, as well as the number of the church my parents attended. Calling their minister first, I explained to him as best I could what had happened. I asked that he go to my parents—not to tell them of the accident but to be there to support them when I told them about Christopher's death. He assured me he would leave for their house immediately; he could be there in ten minutes or less. I then called Mary Ann and asked her to go to the house as well.

When I dialed my parents' number, my heart ached for them. My task seemed impossible. What words could I use to tell them, to soften the impact of this devastating news, to explain that their innocent grandson had just been killed?

When my mother answered the phone, she showed her obvious surprise at my call this time of the day and week, knowing that we usually called in the evenings and on weekends. A morning call on a Wednesday could be expected to raise the same alarm as those other calls we dread so much—the ones that come in the middle of the night bearing bad news of one sort or another. I asked her if the minister was there. In a voice glaring with shock, she said, "Why yes, how did you know?" In that same instant she realized something was terribly wrong. "What's happened?" she asked, in a barely audible voice.

My reply was equally weak, but I managed to tell her: "We've had a tragedy—Christopher has been killed." Beyond that I remember very little of our conversation except that arrangements were made for my mother and father to be on the first flight to Vermont.

We made the same painful call to Mairi's parents in Ohio; within hours they, too, were on their way. Now that these critical elements were in place, I withdrew again into a dulled stupor. The reality of the past few hours surged in and out of my consciousness in overpowering waves of shock and grief.

The most positive thing I can recall about the first day was the loving support we found in those who surrounded us; we didn't want to be alone in those first hours. Both Mairi and I desperately needed to talk about what had happened to us, and I found that I needed to be held physically. More than once I sobbed in Mairi's arms or the arms of a close friend. The entrance of each new person into our home opened the floodgates of sorrow again for both them and us; each encounter was a fresh reminder of what had happened, of why they were there.

Many times when we are faced with a tragedy among our close friends, we hesitate to step in and lend direct support to those who have suffered the loss. We worry about intruding into these sensitive moments and about our own inadequacy to provide any help. We are concerned that we won't say the right things, do the right things. Besides, we feel, they *know* how much we care about them; they *know* our thoughts are with them. We think we need to give them room, and so we sometimes stay away, leaving direct support to others. But who are these others? Aren't they friends just like us? What happens if these others make the same erroneous assumptions we have made? Then the grieving are left alone in their grief, and isolated. Believe me when I say that the loneliness and emptiness they will experience at such a time can literally devour them.

Thinking about your friend's sorrow and sympathizing with him is *not* the same as physically being there. Thoughts are not enough. Saying the right thing is far less critical than offering a shoulder to cry on. Just the presence of a friend's face and his willingness to listen to the retold story of the loss help fill the tremendous emptiness the grieving are feeling. So put aside your own discomfort and go to those who need you. They will never forget the support you provide by your presence alone.

Somewhere in the jumble of those first few hours, there was talk of the funeral and related matters I found almost impossible to deal with. Fortunately Mairi's brother Bill had arrived from Ohio; he gracefully stepped in to coordinate the less personal arrangements of the funeral for us. The help Bill gave is one example of how friends and relatives can truly help the bereaved.

What Bill did *not* do was step in and "take over"; that would have been destructive. Although the urge for some may be strong to assume all the burdens of funeral arrangements and other details, remember that the funeral and the decisions surrounding it are a very personal matter. Aside from providing logistical help in carrying out plans, let the bereaved parents do all the planning they have the will and energy to do. They will ask for help where it is needed, and if you are sensitive and observant, you will read those situations where other suggestions may be appropriate. The funeral should be a reflection of the way they feel about what has happened while also serving as an opportunity to gather together those who care for both the deceased and the bereaved.

Let the parents decide how to dress the child for burial, and let them choose the music for the funeral service. If the funeral does not reflect their vision, years of bitterness, sadness, or embarrassment may result.

As Mairi and I began to piece together the plans for Christopher's funeral, one of the major questions facing us was whether or not Meghan, at age five, should see the body. We didn't know just how devastating the visual impact of his injuries might be on our children—especially Meghan. And regardless of his condition, I was very much against her seeing him; I wondered what could be gained by this additional trauma. Fortunately our family pediatrician advised us that if Meghan did not see his body, she might fail to assimilate what had happened into her reality—and this unfilled void might cause problems in the years to come. Also, there would have been a likelihood of her remembering her first encounter with death as one in which she was simply "left out."

I realize now that to have left Meghan out of this part of the grieving process would have been a terrible mistake. My well-intentioned efforts to protect her might have scarred her for life. I suggest to other parents in similar circumstances that they allow, and even encourage, any brothers and sisters who want to view the body to do so unless there are very strong reasons against it. For example, if the death resulted from some extreme physical trauma, seek the advice of the funeral director and other professionals regarding viewing. Never force siblings to view the body, but remember that preventing them from experiencing this part of grieving will only add an unhealthy element of mystery to already confused and burdened juvenile emotions.

And so in the early evening of the first day, John, Meghan, and I drove to the airport to pick up my parents. It broke my heart when I saw them coming down the ramp—this time not for a simple visit but to help us bury their grandson. In the midst of the noisy, crowded arrival area we embraced and wept. Despite the busy surroundings, it was as if we were alone.

I took them aside and we sat down in a row of chairs along the wall. I let them ask questions, and I provided the best answers I could. They wanted to know if Christopher had suffered. I told them no. I described the accident first, then told them about my cancer. I made my cancer diagnosis sound perfectly matter-of-fact, and they took it far better than I had expected. Perhaps it was all just too much. Perhaps in the shadow of Christopher's death, the cancer could be dealt with—both by them and by me. That was how I felt now, and it relieved me to see them accept this latest revelation with such fortitude.

Another process of resolution for Mairi and me began in those first few hours: the assessment of our feelings toward David, the man who ran over Christopher. As Mairi and I discussed the accident it became clear to us that we should not blame him for Christopher's death. He was, through the result of a moment's inattentiveness, a victim of the accident as much as Christopher and we were. Had there been some obvious or willful negligence on his part—for example, had he been drinking—I'm sure the forgiveness we came to feel would have been harder to attain. So before we even went to the funeral home for the first time to see Christopher's body, we drove to David's house high on the side of a nearby mountain. Through the snow and sleet that had begun to fall, we walked to his door to tell him that we didn't blame him for our son's death.

The scene at David's house that bleak April night was one of utter desolation. His parents were with him, as was his fiancée. When we entered the room where he was sitting, we found him holding his head in his hands, his body shaking with sobs as he repeated over and over again how sorry he was. Together Mairi, David, and I wept for our mutual loss. We had lost a son. And, since he lives in a close-knit community, David not only had to bear his involvement in Christopher's death, but he had to live with the fact that he had lost the opportunity ever to know our little boy. This in particular seemed to hurt him very much. Despite the depth of our despair, our visit to David's house lifted a great burden, both for us and for him.

When the death of a child involves a third party, or even a member of the family who somehow contributed to the death, we should sort out feelings toward that person as soon as possible. While we may not completely resolve these feelings in the first hours, days, weeks, or even months, there must come a time when some level of forgiveness occurs, or at least an acceptance of another party's role in the tragedy. Otherwise the ultimate peace we all seek following a tragedy will forever elude us. If we fail to work through forgiveness, we may destroy not only the life of the one we choose not to forgive, but, in the process, our own lives as well.

Of course, the ultimate test comes when the death was caused by another's deliberate action—such as murder. In such a case forgiveness may be almost impossible. I do know, however, of situations where forgiveness has occurred. One that sticks in my mind involved a woman named Corrie Ten Boom. Corrie lived during the Holocaust, and, along with her family, built a hiding place in their home for Jews trying to escape the Nazis. When their clandestine work was discovered, the entire family was arrested and incarcerated in a concentration camp. To add to Corrie's misery, the Nazis split the family up so they wouldn't have the solace of each other's company. The entire family died in these camps except for Corrie. She later met one of the Nazi officers whose actions caused the death of a sister; through the resources of her faith, she was able to forgive him. To me, this is the ultimate in forgiveness: a family divided and destroyed by a merciless evil, a sole survivor willing and able to forgive.

In our humanness, some of us will be unable to forgive. Such an ultimate forgiveness often requires resources beyond our own. We may not be at a point in our faith where we can draw on those resources. If this is the case, we must try at least to *accept* the outcome—including the involvement of those who brought about the death. We must work it through to the point where we can "let it go" or we, too, will become victims of the event.

When we left David's house that evening, and drove down the darkened mountain through the cold, stormy night, we had no idea how significant this initial step in reconciliation would be for both our souls and his—it went a long way towards easing each encounter with him in the months and years to come.

Our drive ended at the funeral home. How we ached as we pulled up to the curb outside. How many times had we passed this place when other cars were lined at the same curb silently speaking of someone else's grief? Tonight the soft light shining in the window was for us, and it hurt immensely. The director met us at the door and took us into the large main room. The reality of our tragedy hit hard as we saw Christopher in the casket for the first time.

The impact of seeing your child in a casket, lifeless where there had been so much life only hours before, defies description. The experience was heightened by the subtle changes death brings with it. Christopher's hair was brushed in a different way and was matted. We found that we had to rearrange it. Unlike the barefoot little boy who raced around our house earlier that day, he had on freshly polished shoes. Again, we could not help but take off his shoes and socks. Meghan had brought along some small toy animals she and Christopher had shared; she wanted to put them in the casket with a note telling Christopher how she loved him and missed him. Our older boys, John and Brian, were the first to touch, then hold, his cold, stiff hands. Soon Christopher's hands were soft and warm again. Our actions were unfolding without plan but with purpose. We were acting out our grief.

All of this is part of the ritual of death. All of it is acceptable. It is healthy for the living. There are no written rules that set limits for how you deal with your grief. You should express your grief the way you choose, as long as it contributes to your facing the death.

Due to Christopher's age, the circle of those who knew him was relatively small. That, coupled with the visible nature of his injuries, resulted in our decision not to have open calling hours. Our family, however, made frequent trips to the funeral home. More than once we were joined by our closest friends, those who had gathered at our home to offer us their support. Their intimate friendship with us placed them in a position that allowed them to see our earliest reactions to grief.

For those who observe these early responses to death, as well as the deeper grieving that follows, there is the natural tendency to assess how well the bereaved are dealing with their loss. We realize the tremendous stress they are under, and so we look for measures of their success—or failure—to cope. While many of their actions may seem foreign to a pattern of normal behavior, they do not necessarily indicate a breakdown in the coping process. To the contrary: unless the actions are bizarre, they are most likely serving a useful role in recovery.

So be kind in your assessments; be slow to judge or to second-guess. Don't contribute to any idle gossip about the bereaved; comments shared with other friends should originate out of genuine love and concern. They should be followed by supportive action, not just more idle talk. Test your motives before you speak.

Remember, too, that the image of suffering promoted by our culture—that being stoic is stronger, that if we can somehow keep the tears back we are dealing with it better—is misleading. Direct your energy toward encouraging a healthy expression of emotions from those who are hurting. Give them a shoulder to cry on; listen to the words with which they struggle to express their loss. Most likely they will be on an emotional roller coaster unlike anything you have ever seen before—unless, of course, you, too, have been where they are. And if you have, you know the depth of the emotions they feel—depths which they may have never before encountered.

As our first evening without Christopher deepened into nighttime, our friends remained with us. We came home to a house full of loving neighbors who supplemented our limited energy with theirs. When Mairi and I finally made our way to bed, it was to be a distressing night for both of us. Despite heavy doses of Valium and, later, some chloral hydrate, there would be no sleep for me. Mairi slept poorly as well.

In the darkness of our bedroom on that first lonely night I saw it all over again each time I shut my eyes. I heard the screams, I ran down the stairs and out into the driveway—time and time again. My mind desperately challenged the facts. It couldn't have really happened. Christopher's life couldn't be over so quickly.

But it had happened, and it was not over; it was only beginning. I was exhausted, and yet there would be no sleep this night—and little sleep or peace for many days and nights to come.

O! call back yesterday, bid time return.
SHAKESPEARE, *Richard II*

CHAPTER 4

The First Days

THE FIRST DAYS following Christopher's death were a continuation of the nightmare. Even with heavy medication, I found restful sleep an impossibility. This lack of sound sleep, coupled with the effects of the medication, left me in a zombielike state. I only existed; I was no longer functioning by the world's measure. With each passing day I moved closer to overwhelming exhaustion.

When I shut my eyes at night, it was as if I had turned on a projector in my head that replayed the scene of Christopher's death without stop. Try as I might, I could not block the images out. Attempts to concentrate on other things could not erase the vivid image of Christopher lying in the driveway. And so I spent those first dark, sleepless nights tossing around, filled with uncontrollable anxiety, holding Mairi close to me as we both sobbed in the isolation of our bedroom and in the deeper isolation of our pain.

Days were spent in a halfhearted attempt to meet, somehow, my basic needs. Often I wandered out of the house alone and studied the tracks of the garbage truck, still visible in the sand and gravel of our driveway. In my troubled mind I tried to piece together how it had all happened. As I stood here at the beginning of the tracks, there had been life—as I moved along their course and reached the point where they veered into our yard, there was death.

Meghan and I took a walk to the stone wall where the pictures of Christopher had been taken the previous fall. She got down on her hands and knees and, in the matted leaves of that past autumn, found the white tufts of milkweed he had dropped there just six months earlier. She slipped a pod into the pocket of her jacket, and we walked quietly back to the house, holding hands and lost in our separate thoughts.

Aside from the preoccupation with memories, the most immediate and seemingly unfaceable demand was completing the burial. We had decided on a memorial service in our town as well as a final service in Ohio. Christopher was to be buried in a family-owned plot in my wife's hometown. My brother-in-law Bill continued to be a tremendous help in working through the details of the funeral and arranging the transportation of Christopher's body to Ohio. Our friends helped immeasurably with the arrival of out-of-state relatives, preparing meals for all, and, most of all, through having the patience to listen, and in lending the literal shoulder to cry on. They were there, extending much needed encouragement and support.

Christopher was killed on Wednesday, leaving us only one day to arrange the local memorial service on Friday. We planned to depart for Ohio on Saturday. As we tried to plan out the service, my greatest fear was that the church might be empty: the memorial would be held during the week, and we were not natives of the town. In my state of brokenness, I felt that an empty church would have compounded the emptiness I already had inside of me.

When Friday came, Mairi and I found ourselves overwhelmed by a show of support far greater than any we could ever have imagined. The community took us into their arms in a warm gesture of love. Many of those who came had to stand outside the church during the service. And more than one hundred people from my office drove thirty miles to attend the memorial.

Often we fall short in our support of the grieving by making the same assumption we may have made earlier in the support process—that the bereaved know our thoughts are with them. We conclude that, in a funeral setting, we wouldn't be noticed or missed. Just the opposite is true. The people who fill the church are like a soothing ointment on a wound. They represent the physical presence of caring and love, and in the loneliness of death, love is a tremendous comfort. Make an extra effort to attend the service.

With the local service behind us, Mairi and I and our children left early the next morning for the trip to Ohio. This final step in the funeral process weighed heavily on me as we drove through the town, passing the church where, the day before, Christopher's service had been held. As the church disappeared into the distance behind us, a new dimension was added to the total physical separation from Christopher—a separation that would be completed with the second service and burial in Ohio.

Our arrival in Ohio was extremely painful, since it brought with it our first contact with Mairi's six remaining brothers and sisters. The hurt deepened as we were surrounded by them and their children—many of whom were very close to Christopher's age. At the funeral home, little hands gently placed notes and other mementos in the casket, joining those we had placed there in Vermont. Memories flooded over us as we recalled the last trip to Ohio the previous August, when Christopher had played with these same cousins.

The second and final service was held with Christopher's small casket at the front of the church. Unlike the service in Vermont, where I had been too distraught to participate, this time I was able to read the eulogy I had written for Christopher just the day after his death.

I had written the eulogy during a quiet moment in our bedroom, having left the supportive group of friends and relatives downstairs to be alone for a while. Mairi came into the room while I was writing and found me with tears spilling down my cheeks. When she asked what I was doing, I told her I was writing down the thoughts that were furiously rushing around in my head.

Now in the hushed church filled with a few relatives, and a larger group of strangers, I walked past Christopher's casket and up to the altar. John and Brian stood beside me as I began to read the eulogy I had titled "Christopher's Gift."

Christopher was a beautiful but fragile ray of sunshine in our lives that even the darkest clouds cannot dim. His love of life and of people glowed in every blue-eyed smile. In so many immeasurable ways, he gave to us, and to others, precious moments and memories that will live with us all forever.

To our friends, he was someone who brought us close in life and even closer in death.

To his grandparents, he was the reassurance of the renewal of life and of its precious innocence.

To his brother John, he was his hockey partner.

To his brother Brian, he was a wonderful companion who followed him around like a faithful little puppy.

To his sister Meghan, he was someone very special to share the dark of night in their toy-strewn bedroom.

To Mairi, he was the fulfillment of a dream to have a full and beautiful family.

To me, he was the tiny guy with blond-white hair who worried so much about my "ouches" when I was hurt and whose smiles and sparkling eyes melted my soul.

Christopher had just begun to talk in sentences in the last month or two, and he and I had developed some special exchanges between us.

The one that I will remember forever was one he created in just the last few weeks.

He would leave the room I was in, and from some far corner of the house, I would hear his little voice call me.

"Daddy, where are you?"

I would answer, "I'm right here Chris, where are you?"

"Wight here," he would say, and then he would run and kiss me.

And now through the tears and grief I ask, "Chris, where are you?"

And I hear the voice of my tiny angel tell me, "Wight here, Daddy," and I know that he is at peace.

As I finished reading and joined Mairi again in the pew at the front of the church, I knew that in another half hour—the time it would take to complete the drive to the cemetery and the burial itself—all physical contact with Christopher would be broken forever.

The recognition of the significance of this coming separation grew in me as John, Brian, and I, along with my brothers-in-law, carried the casket outside the church. As we slid it into the rear of the hearse, Meghan handed me a picture she had drawn for Christopher. Friends, relatives, and strangers stood silently in the warm April sunshine while I fumbled to slip the picture through the now-sealed lid of the casket. Here we were, with the grave waiting only minutes away, still desperately holding onto this last vestige of contact with our dead son.

The procession moved on to the cemetery, and the final moments of remembrance were shared by a small group of family as the casket was lowered slowly into the open grave.

As I stood there at the grave, the thought that this was forever pounded inside my head. I was only beginning to absorb what had happened, and the most frightening realization continued to be that the physical separation from Christopher would now be made permanent. For the past six days we had struggled to accept the very event of Christopher's death; now we were facing the absolute physical separation from him.

Although we may send our children off to some friend's house for the first night away from us, or pack them off to college with tears, these are good-byes that mark a temporary separation. In contrast, the tears that fell at Christopher's grave marked the beginning of a complete separation from him in this life—one that would forever face us, day in and day out, for as long as we would live.

I remember another painful time of separation; it was when

my oldest son, John, was about Christopher's age. We had left him with Mairi's parents for a brief visit after one of our trips to their home in Ohio. While I was extremely reluctant to leave him (at that time he was our only child) I knew how special his extra week with Mairi's parents would be without us around to interfere. As a new parent, I had never before faced any sort of "letting go"—not even something as simple as a few days apart. The week went by slowly, punctuated by frequent phone calls to Ohio to check on John. I missed him in a way I had never missed anyone before. At the end of the week, I was incredibly anxious to have John back home with Mairi and me. I looked forward to Saturday, when Mairi's parents would drive him out to our apartment in Baltimore. Yet on Friday night they told us, to my alarm, that their plans had to be changed; there was no way they would be free to drive John home before the following weekend.

Quite frankly I didn't handle that news well at all. I missed my little boy, and I wanted him back. Only reluctantly had I let him go for a week, and for me two weeks without him were absolutely out of the question. I thought of a thousand reasons why he shouldn't stay the extra week, ranging from the dangers of the lake next to his grandparents' house to the psychological trauma a two-year-old might experience as the result of being separated from his parents for such a long time. The real reason for my anxiety was, of course, my own longing for him. In the end, I worked out an arrangement that met my needs: we drove halfway to Ohio to meet them. I'll never forget how excited I was to hold my little boy again.

The longing that came with Christopher's death, while on a far different scale, can be compared to that long-ago week without John. I fully expected to have John back in a finite period of time, and I made sure that I fulfilled my need to have him back in that one week. As I stood at Christopher's grave and let go of him in death, I saw that the span of time to come was incomprehensible. It would be for forever, and it was totally beyond my control to make that period of time any shorter. The loss of control was so very frightening.

It is at this time, after the burial physically separates you from your loved one, that the shock waves hit home. For me there were moments of absolute panic. I suffered from anxiety attacks, during which my heart raced in response to each thought of how enormously my life was now changed. During those times, breathing became difficult, and I felt absolutely unable to do anything to resolve my condition. Although physical problems that occur because of extreme grief do diminish with time, they are still extremely frightening; it is impossible to predict when they might occur or what might trigger them.

When our family returned home from the funeral in Ohio, we entered a world marked by a dramatic new silence. Our home, now empty of Christopher's sounds, seemed precisely as quiet as a tomb. Accentuating the silence was the space that opened up around us as our friends drew back to allow room for the adjustment they knew we must make.

While we reach a point in our grieving when we need time alone, the sudden shift from the intense outpouring of support just after the death to the quiet void following the funeral feels much like hitting the brakes on a car moving at ninety miles an hour. In our effort to supply room for the healing, we sometimes go too far. Our friends need to seek a careful balance between drawing back too much and not enough.

Following the funeral, friends often find it difficult—awkward might be a more accurate word—to continue their direct support. Somehow our society has marked the time following the funeral as the point beyond which any desire for contact should come from the grieving. From Mairi's and my experience, I think those who have suffered the loss are often much too numb in those early days and weeks to undertake any such initiatives—even a simple phone call to a friend.

It is much easier for friends to mourn with the parents in the moments just following death rather than four or five weeks later. Yet the parents need the support of friends as much at five weeks, and throughout the lengthy grieving process, as they did in the beginning. While a friend's life may be returning to normal, the grieving parents will continue to be consumed by their loss. An occasional visit or phone call to reassure them that they have not been forgotten is invaluable. Don't step back so far that they feel abandoned.

Even in those cases where friends continue to provide support, the period following the funeral is perhaps the most difficult time for the bereaved. It is when the depth of loss truly begins to sink in. In most cases the activity and demands of preparing for the funeral and burial have left the grieving with little time to be alone with their thoughts. Now, like the marathon runner who has charged ahead at his body's absolute limit for the duration of the race, they collapse in exhaustion at the end. Having concentrated all of their energy into preparing for and completing the funeral, they now find a consuming silence on the other side. Now is their time to absorb the magnitude of their loss and begin to integrate it into the rest of their lives.

With the passing of time, the initial painful hours grow into the first, pain-filled days, and as they do, they slowly build into weeks, months, and years. And as the days go on, we begin to understand how much our lives have been changed.

These are the desolate, dark weeks . . .
WILLIAM CARLOS WILLIAMS

CHAPTER 5

The Weeks That Followed

THE WEEKS THAT followed Christopher's death seem, in retrospect, timeless. Initially each waking moment in our house was focussed on our loss. I don't mean to imply that we sat around crying all the time; it was much more subtle than that. His death and the void his absence left dominated our thoughts. In those quiet moments when I saw Mairi, John, Brian, or Meghan staring off into the empty space, I did not need to ask what they were thinking about.

In my own case, as it had been since the first long night without him, my last thought before sleep was of Christopher. My first waking thought each day was of him as I tried to accept that he was truly gone. I can look back now and see that my family and I were deeply entrenched in a stage of grief that is commonly labelled "letting go." The length of this stage varies from person to person, from family to family, and in some ways it never ends.

In retrospect I think one of the most formidable barriers to letting go is the tendency to feel that we are being disloyal to our loved one if we accept what has happened. I have met other parents who have not let go of their dead children after months and even years. Their inability to do so is unhealthy, resulting in an emotional stagnation that effectively puts their grief on a disruptive hold—one that threatens to become permanent. Failure to let go is a state that—if we don't see the need to break it and free our healing energies—will ultimately result in blighting the lives of those who physically survive the dead child. The life on earth of the one who refuses to give up that child will become an empty and joyless thing, as will the lives of those who need that person's nurturing.

I know a woman whose daughter was killed in an automobile accident shortly before Christopher's death. The teenage girl had been at home and had changed her clothes just before the accident, leaving her skirt and blouse on her bed. When she left the house for what would be the last time, she forgot to turn off the light in her bedroom. More than a year after her death, nothing had been touched in her room, and the light still burned—day and night—just as she had left it. The mother's life was locked into the iron grip of this bedroom memorial. She lived in the past, waiting, as if she expected her dead daughter to come home.

By comparison Mairi asked me and a friend to remove Christopher's bed just a few hours after his death. In doing so she was making a painful but healthy nonverbal statement— Christopher was gone, and the presence of his bed would do nothing to bring him back or to make his death any less real. While the timing of such actions is a very individual and personal matter, the important thing is that we face them within a reasonable time frame. Certainly one must not feel bound to remove beds or personal effects in the first few hours, days, or even weeks—some items can and should be kept forever. But there comes a time when our continued clinging to the things that belonged to the dead child is pathologically obsessive— emblematic of failure to cope, failure to let go.

While the issue of Christopher's bed had been quickly dealt with, there were other, more subtle matters that Mairi and I addressed less quickly. One highly poignant memento was the handprints Christopher left behind on our bedroom window.

Our bedroom faces east, and each morning as we awoke, we saw his sticky handprints outlined in the sunlight coming through the glass. For a while we left them there—painful as they were to see. At the time it would have been even more painful to remove them. One day I came into the room and found Mairi with the window spray and a cloth, cleaning away the prints. Knowing all that this simple act represented, I cried again as I had done so many times in recent weeks. As the tiny handprints disappeared, we took another small but significant step in the necessary process of letting go.

Another instance of how important our children's possessions become in the wake of their death comes to mind. When Christopher was killed, the state police were at our house within minutes of the accident, and they followed the ambulance to the funeral home where his body was taken. When I asked the funeral director about the return of Christopher's clothes, I learned to my shock that the state police had taken them. My confused mind, already beleaguered by my son's death, could not understand why the state police would need his clothes. (I later learned that the clothing had been taken only to spare us any grief its immediate return might have brought.) I became more disturbed when I began trying to locate the missing clothing. After making a series of frustrating calls, I realized that the police had no idea where the clothing was.

In my agitated state, I grew angry with this apparently bumbling bureaucracy. How could they possibly lose something so important as my dead child's clothing? Fortunately we knew a sergeant on the state force. As a last resort I asked him to help us find the missing clothing. To my relief, he told us he had picked up Christopher's clothes earlier that day from the officer who had been investigating the accident.

I drove to our friend's home and held my breath while he opened the trunk to his squad car. My worst fears were realized when he pulled out Christopher's boots and one of those filmy plastic bags used by dry cleaners. The clothes had been cleaned.

I knew then that it was not so much the clothes I wanted as

the sweet smell of my little boy they might have retained. Now every essence, every personal trace of Christopher tied to that clothing, was gone. In their gesture of goodwill, the state police had, unknowingly, eliminated something very important to me.

I'm sure my face registered the deep disappointment I felt, for my friend asked me if I was okay. I assured him I was and turned to walk to my car. Placing the bag and Christopher's tiny white snowboots on the seat beside me, I started the engine. I paused for a moment, picked up one of the little boots, and studied the scuffs and scrapes. Alone in the car, I reflected on how these same boots had—step by step—taken Christopher to his death. The thought was chilling.

As I turned the boot from side to side in my trembling hands, a small white sock fell out of it into my lap. The sock had not been cleaned! I shook the other boot, and the second little sock fell out. I cupped the two socks in my hands and pressed them to my face. There was his smell—the smell that parents of two-year-olds know so well. In the silence of the car, I shut my eyes, cried softly, and remembered. . . .

Even earlier in our family's grieving—on the day of the accident itself—my son John displayed a behavior pattern very similar to mine. Christopher was notorious for the pungent odor that often attended him. Regardless of how often we changed him, how much we powdered him, he always seemed to have not just a wet diaper but a soaking one. From the time he was up in the morning until he was tucked in bed at night, we could track his movements through our house by the soft swishing sound his heavily soaked diapers made as he moved from room to room. The "ten-pound" diaper became his trademark and led to the assignment of one of our many family nicknames which each of our children grew into over the course of their childhood. John was the "little deedler," because when he was just beginning to talk he incessantly repeated "deedle, deedle" (a word absent from even the most unabridged dictionaries!). Meghan was the "little bird" because her tininess led me to compare her to a fragile baby bird. Brian was "Mr. Peabody," after a character on the old Rocky and

Bullwinkle cartoon show of the sixties. Christopher had taken his place in this line of silliness with, phonetically, the same nickname as Brian's. But there was a very important difference in spelling.

He was "Mr. Peebody."

At any rate, on the morning Christopher was killed, in the midst of all the confusion and pain, John made his way to Christopher's room and took the sheet off his bed. The sheet was soaked through from the night before. John asked Mairi for a large Ziploc bag and quietly put the sheet into it.

More than three years after the accident, I came across the bag containing the sheet as we packed for John's return to college. Quite possibly he hasn't looked at it since shortly after the accident, but neither has he chosen to throw it away.

The sheet, the socks in the boots, are all okay. They are not used as substitutes for Christopher. We don't treat them as relics; they are just very personal reminders. I suspect that many closets in homes where children have died have precious mementos not unlike ours scattered about the shelves.

While letting go is not easy or pleasant, it is essential to working our way through grief and ultimately resolving it. Where letting go does not occur, the grieving consumes the mourner's energy, leaving life in a state of suspended animation.

Make no mistake about it: letting go is frightening. We may well face an overwhelming assault of guilt that screams at us, "you are abandoning your child!" The emotional attack is substantial. Should we let laughter return to our lives, or should we continue to grieve? If we start to let go, won't we also start to forget the little details of the child who lives in our memory—details that are really all that we have left now? Won't they slip away, just as the child has done, as we begin to accept the loss? And so we struggle with this problem—our human nature wanting to hold on to every tangible or intangible trace our child has left behind—while inside us a still, small voice tells us that we must let go or we, too, will be lost.

*   *   *

Dreams are one means our subconscious might use to help us cling to memories of our child. I remember how desperately I wanted to dream about Christopher in those early weeks. The desire to dream of the dead child seems to be a common experience among grieving parents and siblings of the child. We want those dreams to buffer the harsh reality we face.

For the first several weeks there were no dreams for me. Then one night about a month after the accident, I had my first dream about Christopher. I was on a dark country lane in a car with other people. We were pulling from a side road or driveway onto a wider gravel road. As the headlights of the car swept the grassy area on the opposite side of the roadway, I suddenly saw Christopher in the lights. We turned to the left, and as we did, he began running away from the car, just ahead of us on the edge of the road. I begged the driver to stop and let me out to go to Christopher, but before he could bring the car to a halt, my son disappeared.

This was the first of many dreams following the same general pattern—Christopher was always out of my reach, and I could never get to him before he disappeared. Those dreams that came over the course of the first few months were followed by more comforting ones that allowed me to hold him and talk with him. Some of the later dreams were exceptionally vivid—I could smell his hair and feel the warmth of his body. When I awoke, it was almost like letting him go again, but I found myself thankful for the fleeting dream anyway.

The most unusual dream was one in which Christopher and I exchanged thoughts without verbalizing them. I "asked" him what his new home was like. He told me it was wonderful. I asked what he did all day, what he ate. He laughed and told me it wasn't like that at all. I asked him what he now knew. He told me in a very peaceful way that he knew "everything." When I awoke, I experienced a new sense of calm about his death and found that I no longer felt the desperate need to dream of him again. The dream conveyed to me a feeling that he truly was at peace and that I should be as well.

Please don't misunderstand me. I am not suggesting that dreams are some sort of medium for messages from the dead.

On the contrary, my opinion is that they are more likely a reflection of where we stand emotionally at the time we have them. The early dreams that showed me unable to reach Christopher clearly reflected my anxiety; the later ones, imbued with a peacefulness, were a product of my growing acceptance of his death. When we recognize that dreams—good and bad—will no doubt come and allow the feelings that come with them to move us toward resolving our pain, they will have served a positive role in our healing.

Other elements enter into our pattern of healing. Music often becomes a form of therapy. Sometimes it may make us want to smile or dance; at other times it allows us, or even forces us, to express our sorrow. In either case, its ultimate effect is both to exalt and soothe us. I found writing about my feelings to be extremely helpful. Whether it was writing to other grieving parents, to friends, or just for myself, it helped.

For example, one day at lunch the thought of holding Christopher again occupied my mind. I picked up a paper napkin in the noisy restaurant and wrote down the words that were in my head.

If only I could hold you one more time,
if only once more on my lap you could climb.
I'd feel warmth of life now gone
and the weight of your tiny body close to mine.

I'd look into the depths of your skyblue eyes
to your very soul.
And in those depths, our souls would join,
and if I could choose,
that moment would become eternity.

With my hands and eyes,
I would trace the soft curves of your cherub face
and smell the sweetness of your silkblond hair.
I would feel the breath of life
as it moved through you once more,
And I would lose myself in the miracle that you were.

I would hold you like that forever,
content to never move again.
I would choose to let the world pass by
while we sat there in stillness, for all time that is to come.

You in your pure sweet innocence,
Me in my world-worn weariness.

The two of us,
together in the simple contentment of just being.

Sharing the elusive gift we know as life . . .

When I returned to my office, I copied my statement of love
and longing onto a more substantial piece of paper, folded it,
and put it into my wallet. For almost four years, I have carried
it around with me—never showing it to anyone else until I
decided to include it in this book.

During the early months, I jotted down thoughts whenever
and wherever they came to me. I wrote on the back of hockey
programs, church bulletins, paper napkins. The form wasn't
important; expressing my feelings through writing was. An
expression of one's feeling, regardless of the form it takes, is
an essential part of healing. For some, verbalization is enough.
For others, like me, committing feelings to written form is
more helpful. I found that writing required me to think more
deeply about what I really felt. Putting these thoughts on paper
allowed me to think them through in a more complete way:
seeing them in script or in print reinforced and captured their
reality.

The important thing for each of us who has lost a child or
suffered some other tragedy is to find a means of expression
that allows us to vent our feelings. The form is not so critical
as the action of doing. Music may become the outlet, or painting, or sculpture, or some other craft or recreation. Empty the
hurt from within you; let it work its way out through some
means of expression comfortable for you.

*   *   *

In those early weeks there continues to be so much to be
worked through, the disruption brought about by the child's

death probably being the most terrible event we will ever face. The child's absence is profound, and we must react to it. By inverse comparison, think how much energy is required to adjust to the physical presence of relatives or friends who visit us in our homes. Think how much it affects the things we do, how we behave and act. Usually the visits last only a week or two, if that. When the visitors leave, we find that we need a "recovery period"—a few days in which we reestablish our normal routine.

Obviously those small-scale—and usually pleasant— disruptions cannot be compared with the impact of the loss of a child. The child had come to stay with us "forever," and now his untimely death leaves a permanent void in our lives. We can be assured that the road back to normalcy will be long and winding.

Healing will begin slowly—and only when we allow it. Our family found very quickly that the extraordinary support of friends and relatives, while essential to our dealing with Christopher's death, would not and could not heal us. Healing is a work of *self* and of God.

I emphasize the word *self* because healing is a choice that we must make. I believe that God has given us free will. In the exercise of this free will, we may choose *not* to heal. While I believe that it is God who ultimately does the healing, it is we who must *choose* to let Him heal us.

No one can predict how long the healing process will take. In the first month following Christopher's death, I struggled only fitfully toward healing. My weakened physical condition brought about by the surgery for cancer three weeks before Christopher's accident only reinforced my feelings of despair, and my inability to sleep restfully at night (sleeping medication began to help only after the second week) further weakened me, leaving me close to exhaustion.

As my energy diminished with each passing day, I faced a new and disturbing problem: my attitude about my own life. Although I was not suicidal, I nonetheless felt an apathy about living—something I had never before experienced. The finality of death's dark veil began to appeal to me as a way of escape from all the hurt. And while I never actively sought that veil, a speedy natural death seemed much less threatening than it would have only a few weeks before.

In those moments, when I couldn't seem to care about life—when a return of my cancer would, for me, have been incidental—I was nevertheless haunted by the picture of my family without me. I knew I must move through this joyless time for them. My love for my family, and my consciousness of their love for me, restored my will to live.

I've talked to so many parents who have felt the same way. One bereaved mother, whose six-year-old daughter was hit by a car while crossing the street on the last day of the school year, confided in me her lack of will to live. The woman and her husband had divorced several years earlier, and she and her daughter had lived alone in a tiny two-room apartment over someone's garage. The child had been her life. Now all that remained were the framed photographs on her apartment walls.

Another woman who had lost two children in a single automobile accident told me she would often look at an oncoming tractor-trailer and think how easy it would be to turn into its path, ending all the pain and emptiness. Her sense of obligation to her surviving family members kept her from doing so until she once again found the will to live for herself as well as for her family.

Many of you who are reading this now know the emptiness, where the will to live is gone. Death's promise of freedom from your burdens may seem to offer a far stronger call than that of continuing a pain-filled life. Many of you will only wish for death in a passive way, but others will consider suicide as a means of escape. I entreat those of you who may feel suicidal to give yourself time to heal. Seek help from medical professionals, from clergy, from trusted friends. Don't let the tragedy in your life feed on itself and spread its destruction.

Even in those cases where the loss of the will to live does not occur, it is essential that we allow ourselves adequate time before resuming the demands of our jobs and other commitments. While being busy can help to lessen our preoccupation with the death, returning prematurely to an activity that is in itself stressful may very well rob us of the energy we need to continue healing successfully. We are also likely to feel some degree of guilt about our inability to work as productively as usual—and our failure to enjoy our work.

When President Coolidge's sixteen-year-old son Calvin died in 1924, Coolidge was just finishing his first term and was on the verge of being elected to a second. In terms of professional achievement, Coolidge was at the pinnacle of his career. But the President's autobiography puts the realm of professional accomplishment and the death of a child in clear perspective. President Coolidge said, "When he [his son] went, the power and glory of the Presidency went with him. . . ."

But as life moves ahead there does come a time when we must begin to rejoin the world. Two weeks after Christopher's funeral I returned to work. After only a few hours, when I took a phone call from one of my agency's employees who worked at a remote location, I realized I had come back too soon. Unaware of my family's tragedy, the employee started off his conversation with a tirade about how unhelpful my under-staffed office had been to him during my absence. I exploded at him, venting the anger I hadn't even known was lurking inside me. When I had calmed down, I realized that I needed more time to regain my perspective before returning to "business as usual." The pettinesses of the business world were utterly inconsistent with the profoundness of my loss, and I knew I could not yet work effectively. I said as much to my supervisor and didn't return to the office for another two weeks.

The anger I felt toward the man on the other end of the telephone line was seemingly spontaneous, brought on by his crude manner during our short telephone conversation. But was that the case? In times of extreme stress our emotions do strange things. Anger often surfaces and then is misdirected. We need somewhere for the energy to go—and so we vent it unexpectedly, sometimes in episodes that shock us as well as others. These moments are out of character with the "us" whom we and others think we know so well.

I encourage you not to judge yourself harshly at such times. Try to find acceptable outlets for your inner frustration. Physical activity is an excellent way to reduce the stress. Take long walks. If you are able to, run a mile or swim some laps. But as you deal with the stress, always remember that it has a very legitimate source. Remember, too, that with time it will soften.

When I returned to work the second time, two weeks later, I found I was better able to cope with the demands of my office. My productivity was still reduced, but the compassionate support of my coworkers compensated for my frequent distraction. Much of my time and energy was spent telling the story of Christopher's death again and again to just about anyone who would listen—and not only in the office. Wherever and whenever the opportunity came up to talk about my loss, I did. Each time I recounted the events, the reality sank in a little further for me, and I inched my way toward a fuller acceptance.

Sometime just after the first month had passed, I felt the beginnings of an improvement in my overall attitude. I faced head-on the implications of my continued use of sleeping pills, and decided that my dependency on sleeping medication had become just another attempt to escape reality. Although initially the medication I took carried me through a period when the loss of sleep, coupled with effects of my recent surgery, might have left me physically disabled, I now knew my need for the drug had diminished. But each case is different. You and your doctor must decide whether you need medication and why you need it. Continually address and readdress whether you're using it mainly to escape reality or to aid you in getting the sleep essential to maintaining your immediate health. Taken over the long term, drugs can actually diminish the quality of your rest.

In that first month I also came to realize one of life's most powerful lessons: that we cannot hold on to "things." These things include the essence we call life. What also became apparent is that death is no respecter of our idea of a natural order by which a child succeeds the parent almost as inevitably as spring succeeds winter. Through the death we have encountered, this fact has been driven home in the most painful way possible. The lesson is extremely difficult. It is one we would never chose of our own free will, but it is one that teaches us much about the way life really is.

Most of us live our lives trying to elude the very idea that death can invade our "protected" space. While we may think we can accept its inevitability, our expectation is that it will come first to a grandparent, perhaps even to us—but not to our children. And we have almost convinced ourselves that if we don't think about death, it can't happen. We turn past the brief paragraphs in the local paper that carry the news of the death of a child—someone else's child—in the hope that we can keep the lurking intruder from our family's gates. We can't imagine the pain. We don't want to try.

But then one of those same small paragraphs carries the story of the death of *our* child. Death has penetrated the barriers we try so hard to erect and maintain between us and the enemy. The loss of our child is an abrupt disruption—a stop sign that jolts us to a halt at the intersection of the divergent avenues of life and death.

And so in the weeks that follow the loss of a child, we walk in territory where we have never been before. We did not choose to be there, but the choice was not ours to make. We learn that some things are beyond our control and irreversible. As we begin to accept that fact, we take the first major steps in the process of letting go.

The importance of this acceptance cannot be overstated. It applies to all of life, not just the terrible intrusion represented by the death of our child. We find genuine peace when, and only when, we accept our inability to control the myriad of disruptive and painful things that mark our journey through life.

To bear, to nurse, to rear,
To watch and then to lose,
To see my bright ones disappear
Drawn up like morning dews.
JEAN INGELOW, *Songs of Seven: Seven Times Six*

CHAPTER 6

Thoughts From Mairi

AFTER READING AND rereading books we acquired about the death of a child, Mairi and I noticed one common trait: without exception they were written from the perspective of a single observer or participant in the event—most often the father or the mother. Never both.

Although each book played a valuable role in understanding our emotions and reactions to Christopher's death, Mairi and I both agreed that a more complete perspective—one that not only included the input of both spouses, but also of surviving brothers and sisters as well—would be even more meaningful.

This chapter and the next will momentarily break from the chronological sequence of my account to offer the thoughts of my wife and children. If you are a mother, you will no doubt benefit from Mairi's reflections. Your children may be helped by what John, Brian, and Meghan have to say in Chapter 7. With that as background, let's begin with Mairi's thoughts.

MAIRI

When we received word that John's manuscript had been accepted for publication, I had mixed emotions. Now the possibility was a reality, and indeed I was going to have to fulfill my commitment to the book. John had asked me to share some of my thoughts in a chapter, and I had agreed to do that. Sharing my thoughts and feelings with John or a few close friends and family members, and even other parents on an individual basis, has not been difficult. To open up and share those same thoughts with people I may never meet is much more difficult; it is certainly another step for me. It shows that, as John has said, the journey is never over. It just continues.

There is nothing in this life that can prepare you for the complete devastation the death of your child brings. It is overwhelming and debilitating.

I had experienced this type of horrible loss before Christopher's death when I was pregnant with Matthew. I had been hospitalized with placenta previa and was aware that my pregnancy was in danger. At twenty-seven weeks the placenta ruptured, and I underwent an emergency cesarean section; Matthew was born weighing less than two pounds. He was surprisingly strong and did well for three weeks, so John and I were optimistic. Then his condition deteriorated rapidly. He was put on life support. Forty-eight hours later our infant son, whom we had held such hope for, was declared brain-dead, and it was necessary for us to sign papers to discontinue life support. Suddenly we were dealing with something that had been a possibility for months. It was difficult and painful, but we had really been preparing ourselves for this possibility from the moment my pregnancy became complicated. Our final moments with Matthew were filled with sadness, but there was also a sense of peaceful acceptance.

I thought then that certainly I was dealing with the worst kind of loss I would ever have to face. Little did I know what was to come. Nothing had prepared me for the unexpected tragedy that took me from watching my son play in the front yard one minute to seeing his limp body appear from underneath the wheels of a truck. It was suddenly over. Not a moment of preparation.

I was the only person to witness the accident. This became a vision that accosted me at every turn. It was there every time I closed my eyes. My immediate reaction was that I wanted to be away from this place, our home, where this violent assault on my senses had occurred.

The days that followed were difficult. Though we were in shock, decisions had to be made. You do your best under the circumstances. Because we chose not to have calling hours we were able to have as much time as we needed at the funeral home. It proved to be an important time for each of us. There had been some question as to whether or not we could have a viewing of the body. John was not sure he wanted the children to be put through that. He wanted to protect them. I remembered how important the time we had with Matthew was after the life support was removed. I felt it was important for the children to see Christopher's body, and although I encouraged them to do so, it was their choice to make, not mine. I knew it would be an important part of closure and acceptance for them. It was.

Brian and John felt comfortable holding Christopher's hand, touching his face, stroking his blond hair, and kissing him good-bye. One of the children pointed out a bruise Christopher still had on his foot from a soup can he had dropped while emptying my cupboards earlier in the week. Meghan brought some special toys and a handwritten note to place in the casket. Some friends asked if they could join us, and it helped to have them share our grief.

Although Christopher's injuries were quite visible, he was not disfigured. After we rearranged his hair, Christopher looked like Christopher. It was important for them to see that, so their imaginations were not left to wonder about the mystery of death.

We had some private time at the funeral home in Ohio as well for my family members who could not come to Vermont.

I'm from a very large family that includes eight brothers and sisters. Once again the open casket was on a low table so the children would have easy access. There were seventeen cousins, ages fifteen years to two years old. The small children especially wanted to be very close and needed to touch and hold Christopher's hand. There was such a contrast between this lifeless body and his little hand, soft and warm from being held. I remember my niece Morgan, who was four at the time, sitting on a small chair by the casket holding Christopher's hand. After about ten minutes her mother gently told her she should let someone else have some time. Morgan told her mother she didn't want to. She said, "I want some more time. I hardy ever get to see him." The cousins had an opportunity to place their "little gifts" and love notes in with their cousin. I remember being deeply touched by the children's sadness and the beautiful way they were able to show it in their actions as well as in their words. Leave it to children to show us the way.

John and I agreed to have Christopher's body buried in my family's cemetery plot in Ohio. My favorite uncle, my cousin's wife Lori (who died of cancer at thirty-two), and my brother Bill's two infants are buried there. They all died much too young, and it seemed appropriate that Christopher should be there with them. The mistake we made was not including the children in the decision. We should have, but it didn't occur to us at the time. I'll never forget out oldest son John's comment in an emotional moment weeks later: "He's so far away!" It wasn't until that moment that I realized our error. Although John and I visit the cemetery once a year, our son John has not been able to be back since Christopher's burial.

My family made most of the arrangements in Ohio. John and I had a few requests; the rest we left to others. We were physically and emotionally exhausted. Our boys later admitted to us that they didn't like others making some of the arrangements for the funeral such as choosing some songs. I explained to the boys there were certain details we chose to let others handle. I pointed out that we weren't the only ones grieving; there were other people who were deeply hurt by this as well. Everyone needed to be able to do something, and we let them.

I knew the first stage was over when, on arriving back in Vermont after the burial, we pulled into our driveway. It was the same driveway on which our little boy lay lifeless twelve days earlier, and yet it was wonderful to be home. The concerns I had about being in this place again were put to rest.

Accepting Christopher's death was not as difficult a task as incorporating it into my life was. My faith is strong, and I knew I would be all right eventually. My husband's struggle was different from my own. I was coming from a posture of great faith with trust and hope. I wasn't looking for answers; I just wanted the strength to work through the incredible heartache and sense of loss. For John there had been only three weeks between the emotional upheaval of his cancer diagnosis and the devastation of his child's death. He was holding on by his fingernails.

We limped through the next few months. We had to get back to the task of everyday living. We had to try to get back to normal—which meant learning what normal would be for us now that we had this major gap in our lives. We weren't the same, our family wasn't the same, and our life wasn't going to be the same. We were setting out on a very difficult journey.

As a parent I had great concern for my remaining children. At the ages of fifteen-and-a-half, thirteen, and five, they were having to deal with what I at thirty-eight couldn't begin to deal with. John and I were barely able to help ourselves; we were probably ineffective in helping our children. All I felt I had for them were my love and understanding, which in most circumstances would be enough. Yet under these circumstances I felt it was of little help. I wish I had had the foresight to give each of the children a notebook to keep track of their feelings; I think it would have helped them all.

Meghan, at five, was straightforward about her feelings. She wanted her little brother back, although she knew that was not possible. Yet that didn't prevent her from saying she wanted him back anyway. I would assure her that I felt the same way, and we would usually share a good cry together. Meghan didn't hesitate telling us how she felt. Since Meghan had shared her bedroom with Christopher, she would not sleep in her room after his death; she said it was lonely. She slept on a cot in our room until she felt comfortable in her room again.

Teenage boys are another matter. Although I often asked John and Brian how they were doing, their answer was always the same: "Okay." What kind of an answer is "Okay"? I felt that our oldest son, John, would probably share his feelings with his close friends, if not with us. Brian was another matter. He did little sharing with us, and because of his private nature, I was concerned that he might not share with his friends either. I'm looking forward to reading his contribution to this book. I'm hoping for some insight.

New challenges awaited John and me at every turn. They started immediately; there was no time to prepare. I vividly remember leaving the house for the first time after we returned from Ohio. I was painfully aware that I was alone. In the past Christopher had always been with me. Any trip in the car entailed dressing him warmly, coaxing him or carrying him to the car, and struggling with the car seat. Every mother knows the routine. I was painfully aware of just walking out the door, getting in my car (from which the car seat had been removed), and pulling out of the driveway. It was such a foreign exercise. My arms felt as though they should be scooping up my child as they routinely had; my body instinctively wanted to bend and pick up my child as it had hundreds of times before. Instead, my arms felt like awkward extensions; they had nothing to do. I wondered if it was anything like the symptoms paraplegics have.

There were many painful reminders the first months. Fingerprints everywhere seemed to jump out at us. Christopher's clothing kept surfacing: little shirts and socks would show up in the never-ending laundry cycle. Although it wasn't long before all his clothes were out of the closets and drawers and lovingly put away to be sorted at another time, I was always unprepared when the clogged vacuum-cleaner hose produced one of Christopher's socks or little toys that had been hidden in some unsuspecting spot. The seasonal cleaning of the hall closets produced several pairs of tiny mittens. I was never sure what to do with all these little "surprises." And we received reminders from the state health department to keep up-to-date on Christopher's immunizations. Our wonderful computerized world.

Several weeks after the accident I was in the bookstore in our village. When I went to the checkout, the owner of the shop said, "Oh, I have something of yours." She reached under the counter and pulled out a little truck. "Your little boy left this the last time you were in." I was completely unprepared. I gathered enough composure to tell her that Christopher was the little boy who had died in the accident earlier that spring. I'm not sure who needed more comforting at that moment, her or me. Encounters like this are unavoidable and seem to happen when we least expect them. They are hard on everyone involved. Difficult though it was, I often found myself in a position of comforting those around me or trying to put them at ease. I could tell people often felt awkward around me.

After about a year things seemed to settle down. There weren't as many of these little things to deal with. Eventually, painful reminders became gentle reminders.

Sooner or later the most difficult question of all comes up: "How many children do you have?" For most grieving parents it is probably the most heart-wrenching moment of all. The question is almost always a casual one, asked by someone who has no idea what you've been through. My heart would race, I would get a lump in my throat, and there were usually tears in my eyes. There did come a time, eventually, when I could answer calmly and without tears. For the first year or so I felt compelled to mention Christopher. I could not deny my child's existence; I needed to acknowledge him. I would simply say I had three children and my fourth and youngest child, Christopher, had died in an accident recently. There was a long transition between the time I needed to answer that way and the time I could say "three" comfortably. Each time the question is asked you must decide again how to answer it.

I vividly remember my first encounter with another grieving parent. We had received a note from a couple in a nearby community. It had been a year since Kathy and Roger's son tragically died in a house fire; they were offering comfort and support. We were touched. It was comforting to hear from someone who really knew what we were going through. Before I knew it, John asked them to come to the house. I was not pleased. I did not want to expose my fragile emotions to strangers, no matter how tuned-in they might be to what I was feeling. I was very apprehensive. But the moment Kathy and I met, a bond was formed. With only a few words spoken, I knew how important it was to be with someone who really knew the immense loss and overwhelming heartache I was experiencing.

Kathy and I keep in touch. I visited her in her new home, built on the site of the home that had burned. We met for lunch before Christmas. It was an important time for me—I was facing my child's first birthday since his death and the first Christmas, too, all in one week. Kathy knew the emotions I was struggling with. After all, she had been dealing with them herself the year before. It was a great comfort to be with a mother who had made it through these difficult milestones. Kathy went back to school so she could teach, and she is teaching now. We don't see each other much, but we do keep in contact. We didn't manage to do our Christmas lunch this year, but I still value the relationship I have with Kathy. It certainly has made me realize how important it is to reach out and be willing to share with other grieving parents.

It means so much when friends and family share their memories of Christopher with me. Last week I was having lunch with a close friend. She had been shopping for a baby gift in the children's department when she found herself standing in front of the StrideRite display. She said she stood there in front of the black-and-white saddle oxfords with tears streaming down her face. For her it brought back the memory of polishing Christopher's tiny saddle oxfords before they went to the funeral home. I was pleased she shared her experience with me.

Especially appreciated are those who risk the tears and remember special days. On December 17 our neighbors, Bob and Norma, always remember Christopher's birthday with a special ornament for the tree. Although we tell them, I'm not sure they can ever know how much that means to us. My sister Peigi and her daughter brave the elements each December 17 to place an evergreen wreath at Christopher's grave.

That first spring we received a note from Newton Baker, who voluntarily cares for all of the flowers in the village gardens. He does a remarkable job, and they are beautiful. Newton wanted us to know he had planted several hundred crocus bulbs in Christopher's memory along the entrance to the village.

Words don't seem adequate in thanking people for gifts like that.

Oh, call my brother back to me!
I cannot play alone:
The summer comes with flower and bee—
Where is my brother gone?
FELICIA HEMANS, *The Child's First Grief*

CHAPTER 7

Brothers and Sisters

I USED TO speak of our family as "the two families." Our teenage children John and Brian were one "family" grouping; Meghan, five, and Christopher, two, fit into the other. Perhaps had there been other children in-between, our family would not have seemed so much like bookends at opposite ends of the shelf. While Mairi and I were dealing with the problems surrounding a sixteen-year-old's needs to have the car for the night or encouraging him to keep his grades up for college, we were also up in the middle of most nights changing Christopher's diapers.

When Christopher was killed, our remaining children had very differing sets of needs that they needed to work through in a healthy way—ones that would allow them to emerge without deep emotional scars. The spread of our children's ages and their needs as individual personalities—coupled with our own needs as parents trying to deal with *our* traumatized emotions—presented a substantial challenge to the unity of "the two families."

Of all of our children, Meghan was perhaps the most open and honest in expressing her feelings. I am convinced that she never failed to say what she was thinking. Although her limited life experience left her without some of the reference points her older brothers had acquired, she didn't hesitate to ask the questions she needed answered. Unlike the rest of our family, Meghan had never seen death before. And now it had come uncomfortably close to her, stealing away her roommate, her brother. From now on, she would sleep alone.

Meghan could not cry at first. The day after Christopher was killed, she asked me in a quiet moment in our bedroom, "Daddy, everybody's crying but me. I can't cry. Is something wrong with me?" I reassured her that there was nothing wrong, that as we go through life we learn through our experiences what deep hurt is. Unlike a scraped knee that makes us cry because of the physical pain, death causes a deeper hurt in our hearts that takes time to feel fully and to understand. Several days later, when she began to realize that Christopher was gone forever, Meghan came to me again—her tiny body shaking with sobs—as she poured out her heart, saying, "I want Christopher back, Daddy, I want him back."

I tried to comfort her and explain that we couldn't have him back. As I did, she whispered softly to me, "Daddy, I think I've learned what hurting inside is now." And so she had.

One afternoon a few weeks later, Meghan was having a particularly hard time dealing with the physical absence of her little brother. With each passing day, it seemed, the reality that he wasn't coming back sank in a little more for her. She was in our bedroom talking with me while I was putting away some clothes when she suddenly began to cry. Through the tears, she said once again that she wanted Christopher back. Taking her in my arms, I tried to explain, as I had before, that we couldn't have him back now, but that someday we would be with him again—and until then he would live in our hearts through our memories of him. I added that even though we couldn't see him, we could feel him in the love for him that remained inside us. Meghan told me she didn't understand.

It was then I remembered something that had happened the previous day. While cleaning up Meghan's room, I had found on the floor a small, brightly colored enamel magnet—the kind we put on our refrigerators to hold notes and messages. Since it was under the bed, I had immediately assumed Christopher had put it there. He often stored his secret possessions under her bed, much as the squirrels in our nearby woods hide their possessions in the nooks and crannies of the forest. My guess was that he had taken the magnet from the refrigerator, carried it upstairs to the bedroom he shared with his sister, and hidden it along with his other special toys and collectibles.

When I found the magnet, I almost took it back downstairs but instead followed a sudden impulse to leave it in Meghan's room. I looked around the room for a place to put the magnet and finally put it on the metal radiator besides Meghan's bed. Now, holding Meghan close to me as she continued to cry, it seemed I knew why.

I left her just long enough to get the magnet. Taking it from the radiator, I brought it to her and placed it in her hand. The conversation which followed went something like this:

"Meghan, what is this?"

"A magnet," she said.

"Hold it close to the radiator and tell me what happens."

Meghan kneeled on the carpet and held the magnet a short distance from the radiator.

"What's happening, Meghan?"

"It's tugging," she said.

"What's tugging?"

"The magnet's tugging."

"But Meghan, I don't see anything tugging. There's nothing between the magnet and the radiator that I can see. Explain to me how you know it's tugging."

"I can't see anything either," she said, "but I can feel it." She had opened the way for me.

"It's the same with Christopher's presence in our life now, Meghan. We can't see him anymore, but we can feel him in the love in our hearts."

She looked up at me as a small smile began to break through the tears, and said, "Now I understand, Daddy."

One night Meghan came into our bedroom as she often does when I am typing. She asked me if I was working on the book about Christopher. When I told her that I was, she asked me why I was writing it. I explained that I wanted to try to help other people who might be going through a similar experience by sharing with them my feelings about our family's experience. She asked me if I thought it might help little kids like her if she wrote down *her* feelings. Would I let her write some chapters for the book? Needless to say, the answer was yes. Here for you to read are the unedited thoughts, complete with "chapter" titles, of my eight-year-old daughter.

MY FEELINGS ABOUT
CHRISTOPHER'S DEATH
MEGHAN BRAMBLETT AGE 8 7/9/88

I would just like to introduce myself. I am Meghan, you might remember me from what my dad wrote. I am eight years old and I just want to put in a chapter or two about how I feel about Christopher's death.

One Wednesday morning I walked into my parents room to say good morning to my dad. As he got into the bath we started to talk. We heard the door open and the sound of running footsteps to the stairs. All of a sudden screaming was heard. It was my mom, she was yelling, "John, Christopher's been hit by a car." My dad jumped and ran. I ran to a bed thinking it's a joke, Meghan, don't worry. But then with fear that it was true I jumped into the bed crying. I thought it was the devil's work. Then I ran down stairs and looked in the driveway and instead of a car I saw a big garbage truck . . . and a bloody Christopher. Then several of our neighbors came in. With them, some food, and a tissue, as brave as I could I walked up the stairs.

WHAT IS HEAVEN

All the sudden foot steps were heard. As my dad walked in I felt a non-promising feeling. With a sad face my dad said

"Meghan, what is heaven? Do you know?" I said "Ya, sorta. Why?" "Well . . . the people on the ambulance said that Christopher didn't make it" said Dad. I knew it would be that. With tears in my eyes I squeezed my Dad and he took me to my Mom in the kitchen. She ran over and burst into tears.

FACING THE FACTS

Me and my parents stood there hugging until we looked like a sandwich. Then my brothers came home with red eyes. Brian, John, Mom, and me lied down on the couch as my Dad bravely called relatives and said "Hello . . . this is John . . . there's been a tragedy." Then he would burst into tears. With faith we all prayed that the phone would ring because our grandparents were not home. Suddenly it rang . . . my Dad let it ring about five times and then breathlessly picked it up.

GOING TO THE AIRPORT

Slowly he put it down. "My dad isn't taking it to well," my Dad said to Mom. My grampa wasn't taking it to well because my Dad's uncle whom I call Hunk had a heart attack a week from that Wednesday. At eleven p.m. we went to the airport. My grandparents were not there.

THE WAIT

After waiting for about fifteen minutes since I was only a kitnygardner I said "We've been waiting about 6,000 hours what if the plane crashed?" Not knowing what I had said wrong my brother John's eyes filled with tears and he stared at me.

THE ARRIVAL

Finally we heard a firmilyer voice call out "Who's out younder?" Then bursting out in tears came a red as a beet Granma Beebs! We drove home with a quiet unhappy family. When we got home there were swarms of people sitting around my Mom. She got up and practically jumped into my grandparents arms.

MEMORIES

We had a long day ahead of us so we hit the hay. All of us had decided to bury Chris in Ohio where his cousins were. The casket he was in was satin. Me, Dad, Mom, John, and Brian each put a little toy Chris had played with in the casket. He was in little green overalls and a dark blue turtle neck. The black and blue marks he had on his little fragile feet were cause when he used to run around the house with cans in his hands we would hear him call out "I dropped a boo-boo! My ouch!" And even when he had gas he would say "My dass, my dass" He also had a game with my dad and he would say "Dayee where are you? Wight heah."

I can't write everything I remember but that is what I wanted to share . . .

In the months just before her tenth birthday, Meghan wrote down some additional thoughts about her brother's death.

About a month after Christopher's death I started wondering why God took him away. Everytime I prayed at night, I asked God "When are you going to bring Chris back?"

Well soon I found the answer to that question, and I didn't like it. I felt lonely and everytime anyone said "Do you miss your brother?" I just stood and cried.

Things have changed alot since I was in kindergarten. Now if someone asks that I just say "Yes, but I'll be with him someday." I used to hope that I was just having a bad dream. The one thing I am glad about is I'll be with him soon.

And so Meghan has found, and continues to find, this and other ways to express feelings and work through her brother's death.

* * *

While Meghan relied primarily on us for comforting, John and Brian were immediately surrounded by their friends. The hockey team came to our house and stayed with John for hours. Other friends from the local high school came to be with both Brian and John. Brian was especially helped by a friend who had been through not only a very difficult battle with cancer but the loss of a baby brother to SIDS (Sudden Infant Death Syndrome) just a few years earlier.

The feelings of our two older boys were much more difficult to read than Meghan's. To be honest, I still find it difficult to assess John's and Brian's deeper feelings about Christopher's death. I know they were hurt tremendously, but I find that they, like many other teenagers, don't seem comfortable talking about their feelings or showing their emotions. Having talked with other parents who have gone through similar experiences with teenage sons or daughters, I find that this appears to be a common phenomenon. As time passed, we saw that, while our boys readily talked about Christopher and their memories of him, discussing his death was a different issue.

I found that the best way to learn about how they were coping was through observing their attitudes about schoolwork, sports, and social activities. I silently watched when they were with their friends. If I had the chance, I'd ask the friends if our boys were talking about Christopher's death. I was pleased to find that they were.

During the time I was working on this manuscript, I asked my two sons if they wanted to write about their own thoughts. They didn't resist the idea but neither did they sit down and begin to write. Later I asked them again, and they agreed to summarize their feelings as best they could. The effort for them was not easy. They finished their sections in the hope that what they share may help other teenagers who may face similar tragedies in their own families.

JOHN'S THOUGHTS

Sitting in my dorm room in the spring of my sophomore year in college I am reflecting back on another very different sophomore spring. I will always view my sophomore year in high school as a turning point in my life. For the first time I had truly fallen in love and subsequently, as first loves often turn out, I was left brokenhearted. Although at the time I thought that I had suffered the loneliest and coldest moment that life could present me, I would be quickly and abruptly exposed to hard reality. Fortunately, my lost love's enduring friendship and support turned out to be one of my greatest assets during the time I was struggling with Christopher's death.

My first recollection of the things that happened on the day of the accident was waking after two or three uses of the snooze bar on my faithful radio/alarm clock. Christopher's bedroom was located directly across the hall from mine and in the morning I would habitually pop my head in his doorway to catch a quick glimpse of his small figure. I don't know why I did it—maybe it was just because I needed to see an image of peace and innocence that was so far removed from the world that we all subject ourselves to every day when we make the decision to get out of our beds.

After the tedious early-morning bus ride, my day was progressing in typical fashion. I was bouncing from class to class protected from the real world by the walls of my rural high school. I had just settled into my third-period French class when a voice penetrated the silence of a midclass dictation asking me to the office. I then proceeded to leave class and was greeted in the hallway by my brother Brian who was also headed for the office. It was at that moment when I realized that something was seriously wrong.

Upon entering the office my brother and I were greeted with numerous painfully blank stares. We were quickly shuffled into the office of the vice principal, where we were greeted by a conglomeration of the school's top officials and a state police officer. The classic line "You'd better sit down" was delivered, and my feeling that something was gravely wrong was reaffirmed.

"Boys, there's been a terrible accident . . . your brother has been killed." When those words were uttered, I felt my soul, as if it were an invisible inner suit of clothing, fall from my body and rest draped around my feet. Then there was a stillness that encompassed the room as my body was engulfed in a bizarre numbness.

I slumped into a nearby chair and sobbed.

"Boys, your parents need you. I'll take you home," calmly and authoritatively uttered the state trooper—who was also the father of my best friend. A quick ride in a state police car, and again I was back where my day had begun a few hours earlier. Only now this place was somehow bizarre and foreign.

The next emotion that I remember feeling was sympathy . . . when I saw my parents (my father who I had never seen cry) oblivious to anything other than my brother's and my arrival and their own intense pain.

Soon after our arrival the house was a teeming mass of faces—some old friends, some unknown. All I wanted was to be alone, so I fled to the seclusion of my room. While there, I was visited once again by the state policeman, who had been the officer on the scene as well as my escort from school. He told me to think about whether or not I wanted and felt that I needed to view Christopher's body at the funeral home.

The conditions of the accident were such that his appearance may have been distorted. I was concerned as to whether or not viewing my brother would scar my memories of Christopher as he was. I eventually decided that it was important— if not a necessity—for me to go and see him. (I'm not suggesting that this is the best choice for all situations but that it was for me.)

It was at the moment that I walked into the funeral parlor and saw, at the end of a seemingly endless viewing room, a tiny white casket that held the broken body of my brother, that the reality of what had happened finally struck me for the first time. For that reason, if no other, I am glad that I did what I did—that I made the decision to see Christopher for one last time.

The week which followed was a type of emotional limbo. My senses had been deadened, and time just seemed to pass in a painfully long blur of "I'm so sorry's."

The next phase was that which concerned the funeral and burial. My parents decided that Christopher should be buried in a family plot in Ohio. When I was told of this intention, I became irate. I was upset that I had not even been "consulted" as to what my opinion or feelings on the matter were. My strongest objections were that Ohio was not our home and it was not the place where I saw my brother grow for two-and-one-quarter years. I was also concerned with the distance factor. I felt that his being buried in Ohio would inhibit my ability to pay homage, through visitation, to my brother. This was one of the major "anger points" with which I had to deal.

I eventually came to peace with the issue by realizing that Christopher was not the tiny, blond-haired, blue-eyed frame of a child that we were burying in a distant piece of ground. He was instead, the joy, love, and memories, and a part of each and every person he had come in contact with during his short life. He was a special place in the hearts of those who had experienced his time with us—a special place that would always be with me no matter how far away he might be buried.

Upon arriving in Ohio, I was completely drained of all emotion. I felt self-conscious about the fact that I could no longer shed a tear. And since it was the first real opportunity for my mother's family to share in our grief, I felt that I owed them some show of emotion, which for one reason or another I could not produce. I was assured by my mother that no one expected anything of me, but that they were there simply to help me. I had no responsibility to them, but this is something I realize only in reflection. They were there for me, not I for them.

I had a difficult time writing this. Why? I'm not sure. I do know that through this experience I questioned my faith and through that questioning, I learned what it truly meant to me on a personal basis. Hopefully my relating these reactions will help someone who is dealing with or has been forced to deal with a similar situation.

* * *

On May 2, 1985, just a little over two weeks after Christopher was killed, John wrote three pieces of verse that I saw for the first time almost four years later. John brought them home with the draft of his section of this book. He found them in a folder he had taken to college with him. They are a fitting conclusion to John's expression of his feelings.

WHERE HAVE YOU GONE?

> I loved your sweet life
> and why it was taken I do not know.
> I must only hope that you
> are in a better place.
>
> And if so, that someday
> I might see your face and
> once again be with you
> to frolic in autumn's meadows.
>
> Your life was so short
> but so full of living.
> You were loved by some
> and cherished by others.
>
> I loved you and now
> cherish the memories and
> the love you have left me
> in your soft departure.

A CHILD LOST

> When I look to that place where you were
> and see no one there, a part of me
> dies.
>
> I ask myself why? But I can't answer.
> You were so pure and innocent
> how could this be?
>
> At one time it was you and me
> and now there is just one.

Although your love has not left
your joy and happiness has.

To where it has gone I do not know
but I look to the stars . . . in my loneliness

because now there is just one.

MEMORIES

Sometime in the future when I am old and gray
I'll look back in time to when I was young and gay.
I'll see you there, your white hair blowing
And ask myself why you were so quick in going.

The love we shared has endured the test of time
If I had a choice, it would have been your life for
mine.

I sit in my room and think of us as we were
But then fantasy, sweet fantasy . . .
. . . fades and I am again without you

Brian, as John had mentioned, had also been called to the
principal's office and was confused by the entire situation.

＊　　　＊　　　＊

BRIAN'S THOUGHTS

My brother was puzzled as to why we were both being asked
to the office. Maybe my father had been in an accident; maybe
it was my mother who had been hurt. Thoughts like these shot
through my mind until the state trooper told us what happened.
My mind was in a total blur. Nothing he said made any sense
to me.

He then told us that my brother and sister had been waiting for
the bus and my brother had been run over. He said something

else about my sister, but I couldn't understand it. I was no longer in a room full of people. I was now alone.

The officer said something like, "Your parents and sister need you at home," and took us out of the school to his car. I tried to make sense out of what had just happened. I was trying to convince myself that this was all a joke, and when I got home everyone would be there and everything would be all right. I kept thinking maybe it was a joke, although I knew it wasn't. My thoughts were now too scrambled to feel sorrow. Not only was I confused and angry at the world, but most of all I was lonely.

When we finally got home, my parents came out the door in hysterics. It was at this point I thought to myself maybe this was really happening. My parents, brother, and I all walked into the house. I needed some time to sit and sort things out so I went over to the living room couch and sat down.

I watched all our neighbors and friends trying their best to help us. That was the one good thing I could see.

I began to go into my own little world and think. I began to ask myself questions about Christopher's death. Was he happy? Was he in heaven yet? Would I ever see him again? Why him? As I thought about these things, I began to get angrier and angrier. It was so unfair and so wrong that he was dead.

I kept on wishing that I could see him one more time. I kept myself apart from others in this little world I had found. When I was in this world, I could block things out—whether they were people, emotions, or pain.

That night we went down to the funeral home to see my brother's body. I couldn't look at him for long. I didn't want to remember him the way he looked now. He didn't look gross or disgusting—he just didn't look right.

When I went to bed that night, I had finally begun to accept that Christopher was dead. I thought about it a lot that night. My little brother who I had had so much fun with and loved so much was dead. He had been so alive the previous night and so happy. Now he was dead. I didn't sleep much that night. I kept dreaming that I was talking to Christopher and then he would change into the way he was at the funeral home and disappear.

I never told anyone about this because it was so weird. The next day I just sat around and wept for my brother.

At the memorial service I was in a huge group of people and still I felt alone. I tried to talk to my friends after the service, but it seemed like we weren't on the same wave of thought. I had put myself in this separate world but now I couldn't get myself out of it. For some reason dealing with Christopher's death was much easier by myself. Although I needed my family's support this was something I had to deal with on my own.

I am not really sure if I had dealt with my brother's death in full, but I had been able to accept the fact he was dead by the time he was buried. I think that his burial was the end of his concrete body, but that was not what I loved.

I had come to many conclusions: I had decided that Christopher's death was not going to destroy my life. Instead it was going to be a turning point in my life. I was not going to let life go by without experiencing all life had to give. I still feel the same way today as I did then. I often wonder why Christopher was taken from me, but there are no answers—only faith.

I still feel anger but it is not at anyone or any thing. I guess I am angry because of the things Christopher never got to see or do. But when I think about it, he must have gotten all of the experience from this world that he needed.

Sometimes I still feel alone. When I get this feeling I like to sit in a quiet place and enter my little world where I can hold my memories of Christopher.

I think of Christopher today as my little guardian angel—the same way he used to follow me around when he was alive—only now instead of me watching over him, he watches over me.

*   *   *

Naturally a parent's concern for the needs of the surviving siblings is great. Ironically it is often the parents—not the brothers and sisters—who need the most support during the grieving process. Although society puts them at the top of the ladder of strength in times of testing, it is often the parents whose actions may seem the most irrational, who are the most broken. The devastation that comes with the loss of a child often severely cripples the parents' ability to be supportive of the remaining children. Their inability to provide needed support only adds to their anxiety, often leaving the entire family with the feeling that things are falling apart.

The parents' anguish is accentuated by the nature of their emotional investment in the lost child. Starting with conception, the father and mother begin an emotional and physical commitment to the child. As parents, they are involved in it all—from beginning to end. And as parents, they also fully expect to die before their children.

So when one of their offspring dies before them, they feel vulnerable and out of control. Their remaining children become frightened when they see mother and father so devastated. Simultaneously the parents often feel increasingly inadequate as they struggle desperately to meet their children's needs when still unable to meet their own.

From Mairi's and my experience, we have found that, while support can be shared among parents and children, nothing can substitute for everyone's working to cope in his or her own way. My suggestion for parents struggling to interact with their remaining children is to be honest about how you feel and about how badly the tragedy has hurt you. Open discussion is far better than suppressed emotions and unhealthy silence. The stiff upper lip does not work. While you should give your children all the support you can, you should also give them the accompanying room they need to work through their own feelings. Let them know of your concern for them, but respect their need for privacy when they choose not to share their feelings with you.

One of the most unhealthy reactions to the death of a child manifests itself when we allow our actions to be controlled by the frightful assumption that, if death has visited us once, it can call on us again. We have all heard the stories about families who have lost more than one child. We know how unthinkable the first loss was, and yet it happened. Dear God, what if it were to happen again?

This fear is natural and will undoubtedly face all of those who have surviving children. Its most common manifestation is the overprotection of our remaining children. While that reaction is normal, extreme or long-term overprotection will drive our children away from us at a time when they need us, as we need them, so very much.

Remember, from the moment our children are born, we begin the process of letting them go, of preparing them to leave us someday. When one of them leaves us suddenly through death, we may desperately try to draw the others in to protect them and keep them safe. Balancing our fears against their needs is not an easy matter, but a balance must be struck.

In our case it took a conscious decision to avoid restricting the activities of our remaining children. Many of us who have lost a child know the weight of the conflicting emotions that must be faced in making such a choice. We all want to hold on to all the things we possess—most of all our children—but we are not in a position to exercise that type of total control. Peace, real peace with our lives in the world around us, comes only when we can accept that fact. Even then, each time our children venture out from us to spend the night with a friend, or to ride their bikes on a nearby road, we are not truly at ease until they are back at our sides.

Mairi and I only became comfortable with letting our children go after several months had passed. At that time we realized that any attempt to avoid life's problems through withdrawal from day-to-day activity was to cease to live. And so as we were working through the process of letting Christopher go, we began letting our other children go as well. We sent them on their way, often reluctantly, with more than the usual number of warnings to be careful. But we let them go.

Hours and days, and months and years go by,
nor does past time ever return.
CICERO *De Senectute*

CHAPTER 8

The First Year

As WE MOVED through those first surreal hours, watching them slowly turn into days, weeks, and then months, the pain of our loss began to soften, but as it softened it also began to deepen. Reflecting on it now, we see that the softening comes from the distance that opens between us and the actual event of the death itself, and the deepening from the growing realization with each passing day that our child is truly gone from us—forever. Each sunrise is a reminder that another day has passed, widening the gap between us and our child's last moments with us. The days become a continuum that places a dimension of time between us and our child, one that will widen until we, too, close our eyes in death. Perhaps the most difficult stage of this continuum is the first year. With it behind us now, Mairi and I better understand its difficulties.

It is during the first year that we anticipate and experience those special moments of life—holidays, anniversaries, and birthdays—for the first time without our child. And then, of course, at the end of the initial year, there is the first anniversary of the death.

Each of these events is another roadmark on our journey

toward letting go of our child, toward our ultimate emotional acceptance of our loss. We have had no choice in accepting the death in terms of its reality in our physical world, but there remains a mental and emotional process we must go through that requires substantially more time for completion.

That long-term process begins almost immediately. Especially painful experiences for me involved my returning for the first time alone to places Christopher and I had visited together. My initial encounter with this type of "first" came as I returned to my surgeon's office for a follow-up visit related to my cancer. The last time I had been in his office was to have my stitches removed—on the day before Christopher was killed. Christopher and Mairi had been with me. Now, sitting in the waiting room alone, I cried softly, trying not to be noticed, as I remembered how unusually well-behaved Christopher had been at the time of my earlier visit just a few weeks before. Watching the passing parade of patients in and out of the waiting room, he had occasionally offered a shy smile to some friendly person before running back to me and hiding his face in my lap. When we went into the examining room, he had watched intently—without making a sound—as the doctor snipped away at my stitches.

Ironically, out of the many examining rooms available, I was placed in the same one where the stitches had been removed—where Christopher and I had shared what were to be some of our last moments together. Because of its relationship in the chain of events, this otherwise impersonal room became very significant for me. As the nurse opened the door, my composure broke completely—it was as if I had just left there minutes before and I could still see Christopher standing quietly at the foot of the examining table. All of the pain resurfaced and any ground I had gained seemed to be crumbling away from under my feet as I wept uncontrollably once again. In a few minutes I regained my composure and breathed a deep, shuddering sigh. Here again was the bittersweet pain of remembrance. The next visit to this office would not be so painful, but this one was because it was the first. And like all of the other firsts, it confronted me with memories that hurt—memories I had to move through, not around.

These experiences continued, varying in the intensity of their emotional impact. Some were more jolting than others. We must face these moments with courage, and allow the emotions and feelings within us to surface. They represent one of the many dark valleys through which we must pass—for there is no way to avoid them. If we want to attain the light beyond the darkness, we must direct our steps toward its healing glow.

During the first year the process of letting go continues in other, more subtle ways. I remember that in the first weeks after Christopher was killed, I was preoccupied with the clock on Wednesdays—the day of the week on which he was killed. I would watch the hands of the clock move toward 10:05, the time of his death, and then past it, all the while thinking through what had happened at each of those moments—first one, then two, then three weeks ago. That intense preoccupation lasted only a few weeks, but on a larger scale, the more significant events of the first year mark a similar sort of "clock watching." The first major holiday we faced was Thanksgiving, but its significance was over-shadowed by our anticipation of Christopher's birthday and Christmas—only a week apart in December.

His birthday was difficult. What does a parent do to "cele-brate" a dead child's birthday, especially when there are other children in the family? Certainly you don't ignore it as if the child had not existed. On the other hand, you don't celebrate it in the way you would if the child were still with you. Where is the healthy balance point, one that says, "He really was with us and, in love, we remember him, but we also know that he is gone"?

As the days moved toward Christopher's December 17 birth-day, each member of our family—silently at first—dealt with the issue. We all knew that his birthday would not be over-looked, for none of us would have chosen to do that. But we also did not discuss the event together—as a group—until a few days before the seventeenth. The decision of how to celebrate was a family decision aided by our already-established "open" approach in dealing with all the issues coming out of Christopher's death. While we had put his toys and clothing away after his death, we did not put away his pictures, and we talked about our memories of him whenever one or all of us felt like it.

I know parents who have found their child's death so painful that they have removed all the pictures, stopped all the talk. Either directly or indirectly they have let those around them know they don't want the topic of the child brought up; it is simply too painful for them to discuss. While I empathize with them, and understand the hurt that leads to this way of dealing with the child's death, I believe that the silence only heightens the painfulness of the experience and prolongs, or even destroys, the healing process. The more openly we can deal with the death, the healthier we ultimately will be. Just as it is often necessary to open an infection to insure proper healing, so it is that opening the hurt in our souls—letting it out—aids the healing process.

Our consensus about Christopher's birthday was that I would spend the day with Mairi, the children would go to school as usual, and we would all have a special dinner that night—together. Meghan asked if we could have a birthday cake, and we did. As we sat down as a family that evening, there were healthy tears shed around our supper table as well as smiles and laughter. It turned out to be a very special time for us. Planning for it helped. So did our basic commitment to a "nonavoidance" approach in dealing with memories of Christopher and his absence from our day-to-day lives.

The same philosophy carries over for the other special days during the first year. Try to anticipate them. Do a little advance planning. Try to minimize the anxiety about the emotional aspects of the day through an open, honest discussion of your feelings. Enjoy the day—together if possible—in a way that "remembers" without enshrining. Yet don't look too far ahead in your effort to anticipate the coming of a major holiday or anniversary.

At the same time, don't forget or avoid a celebration of the significant events in the lives of your other children. It is especially critical to participate in their activities as well. Go to their concerts and their sporting events, all of those happenings where your presence tells them you haven't forgotten *their* importance to you. Even if your heart is still empty from your loss, make yourself participate—for them. *They* are still alive. They need to see through your actions that you care about them—even if the best you can do emotionally is to limp along. Otherwise you may find a wedge of resentment driven between you and them because your pain has shut out their needs and accomplishments.

As special days approach, especially during the first year, it is likely you will feel increasing apprehension and anxiety. To cope, be open to change. If you have spent the day in a set way in the past, spend it in a different way if it makes you and your family more comfortable. Some families choose not to be at home on holidays or birthdays. They may be more comfortable at the house of a friend or relative where memories aren't so intertwined with the location of the celebration. Some prefer a place where there is total anonymity—a resort, a retreat center, any place where there is no physical connection with the past.

In *Beyond Endurance: When a Child Dies*, Dr. Ronald J. Knapp provides a list of ways to cope with the stress brought about by special days. Some of those suggestions include:

- Give a gift in memory of your child.

- Donate money you would have spent on your child's gifts to a particular charity.

- Adopt a needy family for the holidays.

- Invite guests (for example, foreign students or senior citizens) to share in a special meal.

As you consider these possible actions, ask yourself:

- Have I involved or considered my other children in this decision?

- Do I *really enjoy* doing this? Do other family members really enjoy doing this?

- Is this a task that can be shared by other family members?

- Would Christmas (or any other special day) be the same without it?

These are possibilities that may help you. Other approaches may not be so helpful. An acquaintance of mine whose son was killed in an accident in July began telling her friends and family what a disaster the coming Christmas would be without her son. She had several other children, but Christmas had always focussed on the son. With him gone, she was certain the holiday could only be an empty shadow of what it had been in the past. For her, and unfortunately for her family as well, Christmas died with her son. She allowed that to happen by projecting her pain into the future rather than working through the months between July and December one at a time. By working toward an event without preconceived notions of how bad it might be, we find that there are ways to make each new encounter a more positive experience.

Let me offer as an example how we dealt with our first Christmas without Christopher. At the Christmas before his death, Christopher had just reached that magic age where he was aware of all that was happening around him—the tree, the lights, the toys, the special mood of the occasion. His absence this year would leave a tremendous void. Our daughter, Meghan, presented us with an idea that greatly helped to fill the void. She asked about putting up Christopher's stocking with the rest of the family stockings, just as we had done the year before when he was with us. We all agreed with her idea. Mairi and Meghan then took it a step further. Together they talked about the needy who were so often forgotten during the Christmas season. They decided that since we couldn't buy toys for Christopher this year, we should buy the same toys we would have bought him and give them to a child who might otherwise receive no presents. What a revelation! Mairi and Meghan's little plan worked beautifully—for Mairi, for Meghan, and for the rest of the family—giving us a constructive outlet for some of the energy that otherwise would have no place to go.

When the time came to deliver the toys, Meghan and I took them to the local minister, who had agreed to distribute them for us. We arrived in the middle of a Bible study, and the minister asked if we would come in from the cold for just a moment. As we entered his living room, he leaned down to Meghan and asked her if she would mind telling the group of people in the Bible study why she was there. It was one of the most touching moments of my life. I watched my little daughter tell this group of fifteen or so strangers that her baby brother Christopher had been killed, and since he wouldn't need toys this Christmas, she and her mommy had bought some for the poor children instead.

Tears streaked down the faces of all those present in the dimly lit room, and I joined in with tears of joy as I once again saw Meghan facing Christopher's death with such grace. From the heart of this six-year-old was born a tradition that we continue each year as an extension of the love we share together—for each other, for those less fortunate, and for Christopher.

Throughout the first year, we parents continue to take steps like these toward rejoining the world from which we have been so suddenly removed. We find we don't often reenter it as the same people who left. Life looks different now. Some things will never be the same. Many of our values have changed. It may be less important to impress the boss by working late than it is to leave work an hour early to attend a son's hockey game or a daughter's recital. The office parties may lose some of their appeal. We may choose to eat alone more often, whereas before it was important to be with the crowd.

The first year is a time for serious introspection. As the sharp pain of loss begins to lessen, we find it possible to look more closely at who we are. However, major decisions about jobs, marriage, or a relocation to escape the pain should be postponed until our emotions have returned to a more normal state. In *Beyond Endurance* Dr. Knapp talks about one father whose fifteen-year-old daughter was killed. The father made a hasty move then later lamented: "She was born in that house. It was her home, and after she was gone it no longer seemed like home to us. . . . My wife and I decided to move. . . . We decided it would be better to leave our memories behind and start fresh elsewhere . . . we did not realize at the time this was impossible! You cannot discard your memories like an old shoe! They are always part of you, but now we have no place to store them. . . . We sold the only place that was intimately a part of our daughter's life—our home!"

Painful as the remembrances were at the family's home in the time just following the death, these memories later became precious treasure—tarnished by their separation from the physical place in which they occurred. Hasty decisions like this can only add to our stress, making life not less but more difficult to deal with successfully.

Christopher was killed in our driveway, not on some distant roadway. Every time we walked out of our house and into our front yard, we saw the place of his death. This visual confrontation was exceptionally difficult. But since that same driveway, yard, and house held other, valuable memories for us, we struggled with and eventually overcame the specter in our driveway. We are thankful we did. I encourage others to try to do the same.

As we encounter these events of the first year, the important thing to remember is that each of them is a special checkpoint in our journey into the rest of life without our child. The final obstacle in the succession of events during the first year is perhaps the most difficult: the anniversary of the child's death. I remember that, as that day approached, I once again recounted where I had been and what I was doing a year earlier. On both the day prior to the anniversary and the day itself I found myself recalling very specific details of weather and events from the year before. I felt the kind of immediacy and vividness of detail that has survived in many of us who were alive at the time of President Kennedy's assassination in 1963, only on a much more intense level.

One of the things that surprised me most about the days

surrounding the anniversary date of Christopher's death was that I once again found myself watching the clock—just as I had done in the first weeks following the accident. My vivid memories of the previous year's events included a detailed recollection of exactly when various things surrounding, but not necessarily directly related to, Christopher's death had occurred. Although I had not been so conscious of the clock since the third week after the accident, this regression did not come as a total surprise. Throughout the first year there had been moments like this when I slipped back into a pattern I thought I had left behind. Such slips are a perfectly normal and healthy part of the coping process. They are triggered by very specific occurrences—a song with special meaning, the telephone call from some distant friend unaware of our loss, the discovery of a lost toy. These are bittersweet links to the past.

As the year ends, we are faced with giving up all those moments that happened for the first time after the loss of our child. Each of them will now take on a broader significance in the years to come, since we will have gone through them all before. As we have let go of our child in death, we now find ourselves letting go of this special year and its landmarks. And as we do, we realize that, unlike any of the years to come, the first year has become a special entity in itself.

See how time makes all grief decay.
ADELAIDE ANN PROCTER, *Life in Death*

CHAPTER 9

Moving Beyond the First Year

THE FEELING OF separation from Christopher seemed to increase more in the first week or two following the anniversary of his death than it had the entire first year. The realization that he was gone, that his physical presence would be denied forevermore, intensified as we left behind all of those "firsts" without him.

An especially difficult problem facing those of us who grieve as well as those who would offer help along the way is that grieving and letting go isn't some neat-and-clean process that lasts for two months, or six months, or two years and then ends. The type of grief we experience is long-term and, although it changes with time, permanent. Quite frankly I feel that many of us don't want to let it go—but with good reason. One moment our child is alive. The next he is dead. Grief, in the form of shock and disbelief, is the first emotion we experience. In this intimate role as the first companion at our side following the death, grief expands to fill the immense void that begins to open up. In what becomes a reluctant, bittersweet relationship, we may actually cling to it as a substitute for what

87

we have lost. If we can no longer have our child, at least we can have our grief!

In the midst of our pain matters will arise that need to be worked out—problems that, to our minds at least, should not arise at all. One such situation developed when we found that the cemetery where Christopher was buried had very strict rules governing the acceptability of memorials to be placed there. Not only was there a size limit on the marker, but the cemetery's governing officials also had the right of approval over all written material etched on the memorial. Inadvertently we found ourselves at odds with the officials on both issues.

First we. were told that, had we purchased the memorial through the cemetery, it could have measured as much as fourteen inches by twenty-four inches. We didn't like the standard metallic plate the cemetery offered; we preferred to use granite quarried from our rugged Vermont hills. Since we had made that choice they said our marker would be limited to *twelve* inches by twenty-four inches.

We were also told that the committee (although we never knew just who the committee members were) would also review the content of any written material to be etched into the granite to insure that it was not offensive. Our family had already had the eulogy I had written engraved on the stone. Now, after the fact, the committee would weigh the material for its appropriateness.

After a series of frustrating long-distance calls to Ohio, Mairi and I both agreed that, if we could not resolve this pettiness favorably, we would turn the matter over to "60 Minutes." That information was passed on to the committee by the cemetery manager. Of course we were not serious about "60 Minutes," but we really were quite upset by the entire episode. Not surprisingly, a representative called us back very quickly and waived any rules with which our stone may not have conformed. It was put in place a year to the day after Christopher's burial—quite a long time indeed!

*   *   *

This initial visit to the Ohio cemetery brought back many of the emotions that had been with us on that April day twelve months earlier. We took the same deep breaths once again, cried the tears always ready to fall, and reflected on how much our lives had changed in the past year.

Soon after we returned to Vermont from this emotional trip I found a packet of photographs on the top of my bedroom dresser. Opening the envelope, I discovered a number of pictures of Christopher taken when he was about one year old. He was dressed in a soft blue sweater one of our friends had knitted for him. His little tuft of blond hair was highlighted in a beam of sunlight. His face wore an expression of serious concern—I used to call it his Winston Churchill look—as he puzzled over the curious process of being photographed.

It was the first time I had ever seen these particular photographs; Mairi's mother had found them in a drawer in Ohio during our visit. As I studied the photos, snatches from Christopher's life rushed back at me—the smell of his hair, the way I used to ruffle it up with my hand, the sweetness of a kiss from his tiny lips, but most of all the vivid memory of his vital and loving presence. Although I hadn't done so in months, I fell apart. I sank down on our bed, alone in the room, lost in these previously undiscovered moments from Christopher's life. I viewed the photographs through a blur of tears. Once again I had been sure I had reached the point where I was in control. Once again I had been ambushed.

Through more such episodes I have learned that, although the sharp edge of hurt becomes dulled, the hurt itself stays. It moves from the position of being our most formidable enemy, striking out at us unmercifully in the early days of our grief, to our intimate companion, becoming a permanent part of us.

Trying to integrate this type of hurt into the remainder of my life reminds me of an experience I had as a young boy growing up in Georgia. My parents took me on the first of our summer trips to the beach in Florida when I was six or seven. At that age I was frightened by the vast and unfamiliar ocean. Particularly, I was intimidated by the waves that rushed toward me and crashed in a foamy explosion of sand and spray at my feet.

Afraid of the deeper water, I remained near the shore, only to be swept off my feet time and time again as the crushing force of the surf pushed me under and beat me against the sand. I had no power to withstand, much less control, the onslaught of waves. I was at their mercy.

But each year, under the watchful eye of my parents, I survived to return again, older and stronger. As each of those youthful summers passed, I found the waves held less power over me. Through persistence and growth, I found that instead of letting the waves crash down and sweep me off my feet, I could keep my footing and dive through their bases, moving away from the turbulent zone of the breakers. I was able to move into the deeper but gentler water where the swells moved in silently from the ocean depths.

In the swells I was able to rise and fall with each passing wave, keeping away from the violence. The panic subsided, and my effort to maintain my head above water became less exhausting. Instead of struggling to stay on my feet, I could now direct my energy toward the more positive action of riding the swells. Though the water was deeper, I felt more secure and better able to accept the rise and fall of the waves as they occurred. Instead of fighting against the powerful forces of the mighty ocean, I found I was able to yield to them and become part of their motion.

The hurt that came with Christopher's death flooded over me in much the same way the ocean waves had done so many years before. The first few months following his accident were filled with similar feelings of helplessness and panic. As in my youth, when I had been locked in a helpless prison of fear, the early months of 1985 found me fighting against equally powerful emotional waves as I struggled in the turbulent zone between the beach and the rolling swells far from shore.

As my experience deepened through time, I began, healthily, to yield to the pain and let it become more fully a part of my life rather than continuing an unproductive and tiring fight against reality. This change of attitude took time and energy. It did not come overnight. And like the small boy who years ago grew wiser and stronger with the passing summers, I have emerged on the other side of the emotional breakers a very different person.

That we continue to feel the pain of the loss, even after accepting its intertwining with the rest of our lives, is natural. The degree to which that pain controls our activity is what we must work on. Obsessing about our loss must not become a constant practice. On some days it will take over despite all our efforts to the contrary, but ultimately it will no longer be the controlling element in our actions.

Think about it: any significant life experience—good or bad—becomes a part of what we are. The death of a child is unquestionably the most significant. None of us expect to out-live our children. When a parent or spouse dies, we are at least able to rationalize that death is a possibility for adults. Our inability to do the same when a child dies places that event at the top of the list of life's tragedies. But after our loss, why shouldn't our memories and our pain become part of the growth that makes us what we are? Certainly the death of our child will change us in ways far deeper than the new job, the next pro-motion, the more expensive car, the larger house. We find the change brought about by our loss to be more complete, more permanent, and deeper than anything we have experienced before.

Some people won't be comfortable with the change. A ca-sual friend once said to me, "You're not the same as you used to be." I agreed. In many ways I will never be the same again nor would I want to be. Before the discovery of my cancer and Christopher's death, I was very much caught up in the mun-dane world.

Our world has its share of superficial people who have su-perficial needs. These people aren't bad, they just don't want to look at life any more seriously than they absolutely have to. I know; I was one of them. Anne Morrow Lindbergh captures the essence of my feelings in her book *Gift From the Sea*. She writes, "The most exhausting thing in life, I have discovered, is being insincere. That is why so much of social life is ex-hausting; one is wearing a mask. I have shed my mask."

Through adversity my thoughts have deepened, I find that I

long to seek meaningful things. A number of friends have found they can no longer easily relate to me. More and more often I find myself alone—not lonely, but alone. And I value this time to think, this opportunity to be a more thoughtful observer. I still participate in the world, but in a different way.

As we move beyond the first year, the sting of death will begin to soften—if we allow it. Quite often we hear the expression "Time heals all wounds." I believe it is God who truly heals; it is God who gives us the element of time. But while God will do the work, it is our free will that must allow the healing to occur.

As I write this, it has been two years and four months since Christopher was killed. He *lived* exactly two years and four months. He now has been dead as long as he lived. My son's life was complete in twenty-eight months. Mine continues after forty-one years. If you, too, are a grieving parent, you know the questions that haunt the mind: Why is my child gone? Why am I still here? There are no immediate or easy answers. In this life there are often *no* answers for questions such as these. But reflecting on these questions is certainly healthy and may, in the long run, be as important as answering them.

It is still very difficult to think of life without Christopher. After children come into our lives, we have difficulty in remembering our lives without their presence. We have made a significant emotional investment in them, and they return our investment with innocence, trust, and joy in living. When they leave too soon, through an untimely death, we are absolutely broken. But do not forget that we still have the beauty of their lives—no matter how short—to enrich our days.

I find that I love Christopher more now than ever before. It is a love purified by death—a love that grows deeper as I weave the memories he left into my continuing existence. When I see a toddler in the grocery store, I look at him through eyes that extend the love I have for Christopher. My tolerance for screaming babies has grown remarkably because I am now—more than ever before—aware of the beautiful gift that they are.

As my family and I hold high before us the light Christopher brought into our lives, it overcomes the darkness that would engulf us. We face each new day with faith deepened by our difficult times. And in the hope that comes from this tested and strengthened faith, the still greater light of God's love sustains us as the years fall away behind us and we move closer to the joyful reunion He has promised.

Guilt is a terrible thing.
BEN JONSON, *Bartholomew Fair*

CHAPTER 10

"If Only" . . . and Guilt

ONE OF THE most formidable issues facing us in the early hours following the death of a child is the inevitable battle with the "if onlys" that play themselves out in our troubled minds. They immediately torment us with the possibilities of what might have been—things that, had they been done differently, might have averted the death. In the case of a long-term illness, the tendency to be preoccupied with such questions is often reduced because the coming death has been prepared for and because most terminal illnesses don't allow much room for parental intervention or control of the situation. In an accidental death, however, there are limitless possibilities, in our minds at least, that—could any one of them have been changed—might have prevented the child's death.

Our first encounter with "if onlys" came from our oldest son, John, just hours after the accident. No doubt we had all been turning these thoughts over in our heads, but John was the first to speak his feelings. "Dad, I keep thinking if I had only done something different today maybe this wouldn't have happened. If I had stayed home from school, or missed the bus or . . ."

John's thoughts were our thoughts. Where might we be if any one of us had done something differently in the course of those early-morning hours on April 17? My answer to John's question applied to us all. "John, you must remember, we don't know how many countless times before this we did do something differently, something that *did* change the outcome."

As I heard myself speak these words to John, I realized just how true they were. Countless times Mairi or I had intervened with our children—all of our children, not just Christopher—in situations that easily could have proven fatal. Choking episodes when they were younger, the last-second warning that stopped them in their tracks, just short of some unseen danger . . . all the times when fate took them to within inches of death's door and then gave them back to us again. Reflecting on the times we had successfully eluded death or serious injury—usually without even knowing it—doesn't take away the pain of tragedy. It does help to put the "if onlys" in perspective.

Certainly we avert accidental death far more frequently than we fail to do so. In our advanced culture, tragedy remains the exception rather than the rule. Yet it is this very infrequency of tragedy that makes it all the more shocking, all the more intense. And when you add to this the fact that the death of a child—accidental or from illness—is out of step with the natural rhythm of life, the intensity of the loss increases exponentially. Even in cultures where the mortality of children is much higher than in ours the pain is no less intense. Study the face of the Ethiopian mother holding her dying baby in her arms, or parents kneeling over their dead child in some bomb-shattered street in Beirut or Belfast.

Despite our best mental gymnastics, the "if onlys" present a formidable obstacle to acceptance. We can only put "what might have been" into the proper perspective by realizing that the "if only" scenarios are not, and never will be, a possibility again. The human mind struggles with these phantom outcomes, and the sooner they are put away, the sooner healing can continue—or at least begin.

*   *   *

A more serious but parallel issue that sometimes arises either independently from or as a result of the circumstances surrounding the death of a child is guilt. Since children are so dependent on us for their basic needs, including their safety, guilt naturally surfaces when they die. We ask ourselves the question: "Why am I alive; why are they dead?" This assault on the senses and emotions is most severe in the case of accidental death. We as parents often feel that the accident resulted from situations in which we could have exercised more control—provided more physical protection or used better judgment—in caring for our child. We as parents are responsible adults—but even brothers and sisters may feel a degree of responsibility. After Christopher's death, my five-year-old daughter, Meghan, asked, "Daddy, would the truck still have run over Christopher if I had been outside with him? Maybe since I'm bigger the truck driver would have seen us. . . ."

We ask ourselves questions like this because we can't blame the victim. We must find someone else to blame. And so we who are responsible for them take the guilt on ourselves. While the desire for accountability is not bad in itself, we *must* accept our limitations. We cannot control the events that impact our lives all of the time. Although we can accept this "failure to control" for routine problems, when the outcome is severe, we are no longer able to dismiss the responsibility with such ease.

In his book *Jonathan, You Left Too Soon,* David Biebel wrestles with the death of his three-year-old son. He is painfully open about the difficult struggle he had with guilt after Jonathan's death. His son had died as the result of a strange one-month illness never fully diagnosed while the boy was still alive. After Jonathan's death, the pathology report pinned the cause on some sort of virus coupled with dehydration. Although David had already been plagued by a sense of guilt from the unknowns surrounding Jonathan's death, the possibility that he and his wife had not properly cared for Jonathan during the illness and had thus indirectly, or perhaps even directly, contributed to his death was devastating.

David's guilt consumed him. He transferred it to many areas

of his life, focussing on his shortfalls as a human being. He began to dwell on the times he had been dishonest in dealing with various laws, with institutions, with others. Things as simple as the violation of a fish-and-game regulation years earlier now haunted him. He wrote to institutions he had attended as a student and told them of his indiscretions while he had studied there. Any aspect of his life where his conscience told him he had erred moved to the forefront of his troubled thoughts.

From this belated harvest of transgressions, David did a sort of penance for Jonathan's death. Yet the penance—confession and mental anguish over these past transgressions—did nothing to relieve his guilt. As his struggle with guilt continued, David sank deeper and deeper into the dark abyss. He developed crippling obsessive-compulsive behaviors that he recognized from his psychological training as a minister but was helpless to do anything about. His preoccupation with guilt almost destroyed him. It was time and a renewal of his wounded faith that eventually pulled him from its grip. His reaction to his son's death is typical of the negative tailspin so many parents enter into when the death of a child results from events that they believe, often illogically, they could have controlled.

If you feel this way, focus on positive ways to redirect some of the energy that might otherwise be wasted in the pursuit of this type of speculative guilt. Properly used, that redirected energy may save others grief similar to yours. Since Christopher's death I cannot pass a mother on the street whose toddler is wobbling along ahead of her at the edge of the roadway—out of her reach—without thinking, "If only she knew." Many times I have politely intervened in some way. In doing so, I am saying, "I know this is none of my business, but I lost my own beautiful child in an accident and would like to help spare you such pain."

Once in a nearby town I saw a small towheaded boy about the same age as Christopher playing alone at the side of a busy road. There were no adults in sight. I asked the little fellow where his mommy was, and he took my hand, leading me to the back of the stores that lined the street. There on the balcony of a rowhouse was his mother hanging out the day's laundry. When I called to her and explained that I had found her son in the street, she yelled angrily at him and came racing down the stairs, ready, I'm sure, to punish him severely. Before she could, I told her about Christopher, and I watched her anger melt into tears. She stooped down and picked up her son, hugging him close. I know she loved him. I saw her a few days later on the same street as she walked her little boy in a stroller. She waved cheerfully as I drove by.

If we are to survive our experience emotionally, we cannot live life in the fantasy world of "if onlys" or in a prison of guilt. We must instead do the best we can to put it all behind us once and for all.

The resolution of speculative guilt can often be aided by external circumstances. Often there are professionals—doctors, nurses, and other specialists—who will reassure us that the disease or illness would have run the same course regardless of the timing of the diagnosis or the role we played in the treatment of the dead child. We are open to this type of reassurance because we are conditioned to defer to the judgment of the professionals whose job it is to assess the pathology of an illness and probably, too, because we long to be free of the guilt.

Yet while often the things that might have been controlled are purely speculative, sometimes they are real. What about those circumstances in which we are clearly responsible? If we decided to try to beat an oncoming car and make the left turn that resulted in the accident that killed our child, we *know* the death would not have occurred without our error in judgment. Somehow we must live with that knowledge for the rest of our lives.

Guilt that comes from such a direct causal connection with the death is not easily resolved. In fact, it may always exist at some level. The issue then becomes not so much how to avoid the guilt, but how to live with it. In *Beyond Endurance* Dr. Knapp suggests that sometimes the best we can do in the struggle with guilt is to allow it a place in our conscious mind rather than attempting to suppress it. Suppression tends to compound the impact of guilt feelings, acting like a catalyst in an unhealthy synergistic reaction.

While I can say that I feel no guilt about Christopher's death, what I am really saying is that I consciously weighed the circumstances of his death against my exhausted condition and my love for him and found myself "not guilty." In doing so I was able to walk through the painful but healing exercise of comparing the "if onlys" against the realities of his death. I searched my soul for my most elemental feelings about Christopher and our relationship and found unqualified love. I weighed my action of not responding to his knock at my door and accepted my imperfect humanity and my illness as the source of my nonresponse.

One of the most important things to accept as we wrestle with guilt is that *we simply can't be in control of all circumstances at all times*. We live in a complex and dangerous world. While we struggle to fence out danger, we can't possibly succeed in doing so at every moment. We are only human.

Regardless of our actual culpability, guilt is a formidable enemy. Our minds tell us that when we have lost a child, we have failed in some way. But before we hand down this guilty verdict on ourselves, we should ask ourselves one final series of questions: Did we love our child? Did our overall relationship with our child finds its basis in that love? Will cultivating our guilt heal the wounds that afflict us or bring back our child? Will guilt speed the healing that we and those around us need, or will it stop our first faltering efforts made in that direction?

Less than thirty minutes before Christopher was killed, he knocked at my closed bedroom door, crying and wanting to come in. I lay in bed, exhausted physically and emotionally from my surgery for cancer. My weariness kept him out. Perhaps he would have lived had I let him in; I will never know.

But more important at this point is what I do know: what I did or didn't do on that morning in April of 1985 wasn't the result of a lack of love for Christopher, and I feel no guilt in the circumstances surrounding those fateful moments. By the same token, Mairi, who let him outside to play and who was watching him through the window when he darted from her view toward our driveway, could have destroyed herself with guilt. After all, she had made the decision to let him go outside. Had she not done so, he might have lived. But she did let him out, and because I know we shared the same unconditional love for him, there is no guilt.

Another factor that both Mairi and I agree contributed to our successful resolution of potential guilt was the realization in the first weeks following the accident that this tragic incident in our lives would lead us down only one of two very different and diverging paths. Either it would destroy us—individually or as partners—or we would somehow grow from it. Many times we discussed how much deeper our tragedy would be if we allowed it to destroy us. We would have lost not only Christopher but everything that had brought us to the point where he left our lives.

So, with the little physical and emotional energy remaining after those first weeks, Mairi and I resolved to fight such destruction. In doing so we focussed on reaching ahead for the positive rather than looking back at the negative. The going was not particularly easy, but we were able to move slowly in the right direction—sometimes two steps forward, one step back—but always trying to move ahead.

Guilt is a most unusual commodity. We don't always have to possess it. We may also project it onto others in the form of blame. It would have been easy to transfer any of the potential guilt Mairi and I might have felt to the man who ran over Christopher. Yet as I discussed earlier, we saw the importance of resolving our relationship with David, for his peace and ours. Yes, it would have been convenient to blame him for the accident. But both Mairi and I agreed that we could not blame him. Although we did not, there was still the somewhat awkward aspect of unexpected encounters in the small town in which we all lived. Each encounter would serve as a blunt reminder of how dramatically our lives had changed on that cold April day in 1985.

I knew that we would meet—in the grocery store, at the local beverage store, at any of the dozens of public places where people's paths cross—and that we must meet as comfortably as possible. Moreover, I felt a real burden to put David's mind at ease about any guilt he might feel. Several times I went to see him. We had some good talks, a few good cries, and ultimately an easier time when we did meet on the streets of our small town.

Still, there were painful moments. Once I had stopped at a red light at the local shopping plaza. Opposite me on the other side of the intersection was the truck that had run over Christopher. For the duration of the light I sat uncomfortably, rethinking how much that vehicle had changed my life. As David and I exchanged awkward eye contact, I felt sure he was experiencing thoughts not unlike my own.

When third parties are involved in death, contact with them may be minimized by the circumstances of where you live; frequent contact is much less likely in a large metropolitan area than in a small rural town in Vermont. But whether contact is a question or not, resolving feelings about that party's role in the death can be a serious matter. Depending on the circumstances, it may be very difficult to resolve those feelings. Sometimes the degree of negligence—for example, drunk driving—may simply be too high to allow immediate forgiveness. And in this world there will often be lawsuits that seek to make things "even"—to offset the loss. Although they may resolve legal responsibility for the circumstances surrounding a death, they cannot heal the soul. Only you can work through these deeper underlying issues. If they are not ultimately resolved, they can be crippling.

Sometimes guilt or "projected guilt" may transform itself into anger. Certainly anger is a legitimate emotion when a life has been lost through an accident or disease. There is a feeling of being cheated, of a future snatched from our hands. One particular memory I have of extreme anger stemming from an accidental death involves a family I corresponded with in a nearby state.

It was January 1986, the day following the explosion of the space shuttle Challenger. I was reading about the disaster in a newspaper from a major East Coast city. I was particularly caught up in the tragic accident because the pilot of the shuttle, Mike Smith, had been in my company at the Naval Academy; for three years we lived only a few doors apart in the academy's massive dorm, Bancroft Hall.

As I folded the paper to put it away, I saw a heartbreaking headline tucked in a corner on the back page of the state and local section. The headline told of the deaths of two young girls run over by school buses—both on the same day, both just miles apart. As I read the account of each accident, I was moved to share our loss and thoughts on healing with the two families. I wrote to each, extending our concern, telling them that it does get easier, that the pain softens with passing time.

About a week later the phone rang. As I answered it, I quickly realized that the unfamiliar voice on the other end was the father of one of the girls who had been killed. He began by thanking me for my letter and then described in great detail the accident that had killed his daughter. I listened without saying a word, knowing this recounting of the details of the accident was important for working through the hurt.

The remainder of our conversation turned out to be a tirade from the broken father—a tirade about the suits that would be filed: against the driver, against the bus company, against the school system. The man's anger was immense. It became obvious anger had totally consumed him, blocking out other emotions so critical to the expression of grief. The healing, cleansing expression of grief—through tears, through comforting embraces shared with family and friends—was being held at arm's length by his rage.

There was nothing I could do to redirect him during our conversation, but I mailed him a small booklet on grieving that we had found helpful. It focussed on moving beyond anger to those aspects of coping that heal rather than destroy. Each parent must chart his or her own course in this unwanted, distressing journey. My prayer was that this distraught father's course would soon lead him into more peaceful waters.

*   *   *

Guilt may arise as the legacy of a suicide, one of the most difficult of the death experiences to sort out. Here was a conscious decision by the deceased child—based on factors we may never know—to take his own life. Even worse, if the factors that played into the decision are known—often they are provided in a suicide note—we may well be faced with seemingly unbearable revelations. Since we have only one side of the picture—the deceased child's—there is no chance to discuss it. He has left us with the pain of his death and the agony of unresolved issues between us. Perhaps he even blames us for our failure to recognize or ease his struggle, and indicates our shortcomings as his reason for taking his life.

Again, we must step back and remember that *it was the child who decided that the only answer to his problems was death.* Those of us who choose to live face the same types of problems every day. We do our best to cope. So, painful as it is, we must allow the responsibility to rest with the dead child. For those parents who find resolution of this issue difficult, please seek support from a counsellor or minister.

In her book *The Bereaved Parent*, Harriet Sarnoff Schiff further relates the thoughts of a psychiatrist and former suicide-prevention center director on this matter. In it, the doctor observes that, along with the feelings of guilt that accompany a suicide, parents harbor an unconscious resentment toward the child for having "electively and publicly" abandoned them through death. The dead child's decision points an accusing finger at those left behind, implying that the love and support they offered was not enough. The doctor also takes a hard line on the responsibility for suicide—placing it with the one who chose to take his life and thus "copped out." His viewpoint is painfully blunt—but it is also the truth.

A short time after Christopher's death, I met a woman whose son had left home and joined the military in an effort to straighten out his life. The mother was a single parent and had supported her son with every ounce of her energy throughout his continued search for himself. The son was stationed at a military base a considerable distance from the woman's home;

their contact with each other was, for the most part, limited to an occasional long-distance phone call.

Despite the fact that the son's life picture was slowly coming into better focus, there were still ups and downs and bumps in the road he was travelling. Late one evening the mother and son discussed some issue on which they disagreed. The conversation degenerated into a verbal confrontation and ended abruptly without resolving the problem from which the argument had developed.

This same scenario had been played out many times before. It was nothing new. But this time there would be a critical difference. Some time before dawn the following morning, the mother was awakened by another call. An unfamiliar voice informed her of an accident involving her son. He was dead— killed when his car left the road and struck a tree. It had happened only hours after the angry conversation with his mother.

Aside from the incredible surge of panic and disbelief that swept over her as she tried to absorb her son's death, a shroud of guilt dropped immediately and heavily over the woman's spirit. Had her last conversation with her son triggered his death? Had he hung up the phone and in a fit of rage driven off to his death? Was it actually a suicide? How could she live with the fact that his last words with her were spoken in anger?

We talked about these and other questions at length. I asked her to think back on her relationship with her son. Had they fought before? "Yes." Were those encounters ultimately resolved in a loving way? "Yes, they were." When were they resolved? "Usually in a matter of a few hours, a day or two at the most." I asked her if it was likely that this last conflict would have been resolved in the same way. There was no doubt in her mind that it would have been.

More importantly, I asked why was there conflict in the first place. Did it come from ill feeling toward her son, or did it come from her love and concern from him? Despite the fact that this last conversation had ended in frustration and anger, its basis was love.

As the mother considered these and other questions, over

time she gradually was better able to resolve her feelings of guilt. Of course, an element of regret remained. We would rather our last conversations and words with the deceased be a kind exchange. Unfortunately life doesn't always work that way.

I can't help but regret that I didn't get out of bed and let Christopher in my room on the day he was killed. The accident might still have occurred, but at least I would have had one last opportunity to see him alive, to talk to him, to touch him. It didn't happen that way. While I missed that last opportunity, I have worked very hard at focussing my thoughts on the other, gentler moments we did have together in his two years and four months. I fill part of the void he left behind with that positive approach, not with time spent regretting what I did or didn't do on the day of his death.

Perhaps some of the potential guilt Mairi and I might have felt was diffused by our circumstances at the time Christopher was killed. Perhaps the fact that we were already reeling under the blow of my cancer diagnosis, that we were both physically and emotionally drained, helped us forgive ourselves very quickly for any part we had in the sequence of events that led to Christopher's death. Certainly Mairi could have blamed me. I could have blamed her. But we didn't blame each other or anyone else.

Further, we have come to trust God for both the good *and* the bad times of our lives. We are able to look at Christopher's death as a painful but acceptable part of God's plan. This is really the ultimate source for resolution of guilt. Through the recognition of God's love, Mairi and I have found we may learn to forgive ourselves and others as well.

They dream in courtship, but in wedlock wake.
POPE, *The Wife of Bath*

CHAPTER 11

Stress on the Marriage

IN THE EARLY weeks following Christopher's death, both Mairi and I saw that we were dealing with our tragedy very differently. For the first time in our married life, we were unable to compromise our feelings to accommodate each other because we were trying to deal successfully with our own individual needs.

Mairi is by nature a very private person. I am an extrovert. With Christopher's death, Mairi's need for privacy deepened and my extroverted nature became more exaggerated. The feelings and experiences I chose to impart to friends were to Mairi very private and personal matters.

One evening during the summer following Christopher's death, we were at a Rotary party. As the party wore on people began to cluster in groups of three or four, exchanging small talk. Mairi was in the kitchen with some of her friends; I had ended up out on the deck in a group of people who had chosen the night air over the noisy conversation that filled the house.

The talk turned to our great loss, as it often did when we were with friends during the early months following the accident. Someone asked how we were doing and, as part of this discussion, talk of the unusual "coincidences" surfaced. (These coincidences are discussed later in Chapter 15, "Thoughts on Faith.") I saw the question as an opportunity to share the growing reality of God's interaction in my life. As we moved deeper into the discussion of these special events, I saw Mairi staring out at me from the sliding door leading to the deck.

I knew what she was thinking; she knew what I was talking about. I wanted to communicate my experience; it was part of my way of coping. She felt that talking about those striking episodes in our family's life cheapened them. She recognized how special they were, and her private nature conflicted with my openness about them. Neither of us was wrong; our approaches were just different.

In the past when we had differed on an issue, there was always a point of compromise, a middle ground where we could meet. Suddenly compromise was extremely difficult, if not impossible. We each desperately needed to be ourselves in expressing our emotions and thoughts. Because we handled the coping process very differently, we began to find ourselves in open conflict over these differences.

This conflict fueled our distraught emotions—emotions that were already stressed to the limit. The result was terrifying. I reached the point where I didn't know how much more I could—or wanted—to take. Mairi and I moved further apart, the gulf between us ever-widening. We discussed our conflicting needs again and again, realizing we must follow our own individual courses, while showing as much sensitivity to each other's feelings as possible. Yet understanding this premise was much easier than accepting it and putting it into practice. Compromise seemed essential but at the same time impossible. We were each fighting for emotional survival, and like two drowning swimmers, we could do little to help each other.

Likewise, communication with others outside the family—especially other grieving parents—became a particular problem between Mairi and me. Quite often I would write to other parents who had lost children. At the beginning, I asked Mairi if she wanted to add something to the notes I would send. I would leave the unfinished letter at home for a few days, awaiting Mairi's comments. Usually there would be no input. The letter would be untouched. It wasn't that Mairi didn't care about the grief of others; it was just that she didn't need to respond in this form of outreach the way I did. It was therapeutic for me, not for her.

Eventually I decided it would be easier just to write the notes by myself. I understood that my personality was anxious—almost compelled—to reach out; hers was not. Yet a crisis would arise when a reply arrived to one of my notes. I think Mairi felt I had evaded her intentionally. I'm sure she felt threatened, as I seemed to be pulling away from her and her needs in a direction she did not want or need to go. Looking back, I can see now that I was obsessed with this contact with other grieving parents. But it worked for me—and, I hope for some of those with whom I communicated.

This letter writing was only one of many sources of confrontation. Unfortunately there were more, differences that were buried under the surface of day-to-day activity. They were unleashed in those quiet moments at bedtime when we both would have benefited so much from sleep or intimacy.

Issues between us accumulated for days at a time—too painful to resolve at the time they occurred, yet too important to forgive or forget. And so, late at night once, twice, or several times a week, the buried problems would surface in the darkness and silence of our bedroom. The scene was almost always the same: there would be a sense of alienation as we prepared for bed—no eye contact, no small talk. The lights would be turned off, and a deep hush would settle over us in the darkened room. Then it would come. Suddenly our pain would pour out, shattering the silence of our bedroom. Either Mairi or I—depending on who was stressed the most—would literally cry out in the darkness, "We have to talk!" The reply would usually go something like, "I thought we *were* talking, I thought we agreed. . . ."

Lying there in the dark, we knew we had not yet really accepted the frightening differences in our coping methods. What followed was an almost panicky, often angry exchange about our failure to meet and respect the needs of the other suffering partner. I dreaded these moments—not because we didn't need to talk but because of the place and time in which they seemed to surface in our disrupted lives. For my part, I needed rest. On those weary nights when the discussions were over, there was no rest. The intimacy of our bedroom, which had always been our haven, was destroyed.

These highly emotional conflicts do not always arise from major issues. The day-to-day nuts and bolts of life—things like messy rooms, dirty dishes on the counter, toys left in the yard—all become catalysts for conflict.

After Christopher's death I found that my main goal was somehow to surround myself with peace and harmony as we lived out our dramatically changed family life. I became very tolerant of clutter in our children's rooms and of other things that Mairi continued to find unacceptable. She was still a mother, and she needed to maintain order in our home. Her nerves, like mine, were honed to a sharp edge, and more than once she would erupt about something I found insignificant and irritating. When the dispute arose, I cringed inside and sometimes tried to point out how much friction and disharmony she was creating. In my shortsightedness, I wanted only peace and quiet—at any costs. Mairi's actions were normal; my reactions were normal. We were both stressed to our limits.

What we did was find a local clergyman who seemed to be an excellent sounding board for the problems arising from our different coping methods. He would listen to us intently, then offer his assessment of our individual strengths and shortcomings related to each issue. Although we saw him less than five times, he played a significant role in the resolution of the stress that had developed between us as a result of Christopher's death.

One example of the counsel he offered involved the issue of the neatness of our children's rooms. While this may seem trivial, it is typical of those things that eat away at the ability of each partner to cope with the cumulative stress.

As we sat in the study of his small house, Mairi explained how she felt about the need for order in our children's rooms.

I supported order, I responded, but not at the expense of household harmony. The minister smiled as he explained how he was very much like Mairi—how he also liked clean, neat rooms. But he offered that not all people were like him and Mairi, and that there had to be a point of reasonable compromise. He also saw the importance of private space for each of our boys.

To meet Mairi's needs, he suggested that she accept the concept that the boys' rooms were their territory. If the cluttered condition bothered her, she should shut the door, visually blocking out the clutter. He added, however, that when the clutter added to Mairi's workload—for example, clean clothes lost in the mess—she had every right to expect and demand better cooperation.

His advice was sound. It worked and was one more small step on the road to recovery for us.

When a child has died, small issues become big issues. Taut nerves are stretched to the breaking point. It takes very little to snap them. We may find ourselves lashing out at those we love most in our misdirected anger and emotional confusion. Often our surviving children become the object of our wrath. The remaining brothers and sisters will not suddenly begin to behave like adults. The toothpaste tube will still get squeezed the wrong way. They will still be children—children who, more than ever, need our love, affection, and understanding. We parents must do our best to release the anger in ways that don't hurt others—especially those in our family. When we lash out at those around us, what we are really saying is that we want everything to be all right again. What we find is that it won't be—not for some time to come.

Conflicting needs are present in every marriage. They range from how we will discipline our children, to how much time one partner or the other spends on activities outside the home and the marriage, to a variety of lesser and greater issues. Under normal circumstances these issues are irritating, but, nonetheless, manageable. When we add the trauma of losing a child to our differences, these small matters become demons that rise up and attack us at our weakest moments. They rob us of sleep, and they tear away at our marriages. They scrape at our jangled nerves, leaving them exposed and raw. If they could, they would ultimately destroy us.

The growing alienation between parents I have described is common following the loss of a child. Statistics show that within one year of the death of a child 75 percent of the affected marriages are in serious trouble. Of these a very high percentage end in divorce. Had I read these statistics before Christopher's death, I no doubt would have considered them a gross exaggeration. Now, from our own experience, I believe them.

The difference between those who end up divorcing and those who don't is the level of the partners' commitment to the marital union and all that it represents. Mairi and I have always considered our marriage a strong one; it has survived a wide range of tests in our twenty years together. There is no question that Christopher's death was the ultimate test of our bond—one that took us on a disturbing journey to the very depths of our souls. We found our capacity to accept each other stretched to the limit. With all of the pretense stripped away, we saw how different we were from one another. The test before us was whether we could accept the differences, adding them to our knowledge of each other, rather than allowing them to destroy our relationship. *We survived the test because we made the conscious decision that we wanted our marriage to survive.* It was our choice and ours alone.

I can assure you that there were moments for both of us when it would have seemed so much easier just to walk away from it all; moments when we were weary and frightened as we tried to cope. But our commitment to our marriage and to our family led us through the darkest moments, and, as the weeks turned into months, we found we were both able to soften our extremes.

How did we both change and resolve these differences? Mairi slowly became more open. I became more sensitive about the things she considered personal. Through our love, we survived. In this process we learned a great deal about a deeper form of love—one that "bears all things, endures all things."

I am convinced these severe tests temper a relationship—strengthening it in the long run—if we commit to sustaining it. Without commitment—commitment made mutually and expressed rather than simply assumed—a relationship will shatter like once-beautiful crystal, never to be restored again. Over the months, we found better ways to resolve our differences. Let me discuss a few that worked well for us.

- Find a neutral place to discuss your differences. Don't do it late at night in your bedroom. Go somewhere away from your home, especially if you have surviving children at home. Fight the battles and the wars in someone else's "country." Anywhere you can talk openly without outside interference is preferable to your home, since it is also likely to be your place of refuge. A spontaneous desire to discuss something immediately won't always make this possible, but, as much as circumstances permit, avoid using your home as your place of resolution.

- Find a neutral third party to mediate issues involving differences in the way you as partners may be dealing with the death and its effects. This mediator should be someone you both trust, not necessarily a close friend, but someone who is a good listener and whose judgment is sound, whose advice is practical.

- Share your feelings with each other regardless of how different they may be. Without this type of communication your relationship will weaken and you will move further and further apart. Like children who must take unpleasant-tasting medicine to get well, we must talk about the differences in our feelings so that we can work through them and find a healing compromise.

The differences Mairi and I experienced in the way we approached the coping process are common. Our exposure to other parents who have lost children confirms that such differences are the rule, not the exception, among bereaved parents. The most frightening aspect of all of this is that we may, for the first time in the relationship, see a side to our partner we have never seen before.

At times we may well feel as though we are living with a stranger. The temptation to give up on the marriage as we endure our suffering may be strong. Our souls, aching after life's most devastating assault, may cry to us that they can take no more. It seems intolerable that we must endure the stress of marital differences when the self within us is simply struggling to survive. The loss of our child is more than enough grief to handle. If and when we feel this way, we must remember that the child we both miss so much—who grew from our mutual love and gave it back to us for the short time he was with us—came from this same marriage. We must be patient with each other. We must try to reach compromises which give our spouses the room to heal. We must talk with others who have been through the same type of experience and have survived it together. Draw strength from their successes, learn from their failures. But don't throw it all away. Those who do only deepen the tragedy.

I never wanted our marriage to end, yet there were times when it seemed impossible we would survive another day. In my most desperate moments I took a mental trip back through the seventeen years Mairi and I had spent together, until I saw her again as the carefree college girl I had dated during my last year at Annapolis. I would then move forward through the years, reliving our experiences together, and marking the arrival of each of our children: John's difficult breech birth, the equally difficult pregnancy that gave us Brian, the loss of Matthew after another nightmare pregnancy, Meghan's birth many years later, and then Christopher's.

Once again I saw the pain and physical suffering Mairi had endured so willingly and patiently to have our children. Her pregnancies were always difficult and punctuated with complications, yet she had never complained. I also remembered the many times she had stood with me as I was going through some disruptive life passage. Her strength was nothing short of remarkable. It made me realize we could, and must, reconcile the stress created by the diverging ways we were trying to deal with Christopher's death.

While we had both changed since those first days together more than seventeen years ago, the good experiences, the good times shared in love, far outweighed the bad.

Underneath all the hurt, she was the same loving person I had married on that hot June day in 1968. Underneath the weariness of the stress-filled present, I, too, was the same person who had told that beautiful young woman at the Naval Academy late one spring night, as we dreamt of our future together, "If we marry, it is forever."

With that foundation and commitment behind us, we struggled, we wept, and we grew. Most importantly, we *and* our marriage survived. Those who, like us, put forth a similar effort will be rewarded with a richer, fuller relationship—one tempered, not broken, by the loss of a child.

> "In prosperity our friends know us; in adversity
> we know our friends."
> CHURTON COLLINS, *Aphorisms*

CHAPTER 12

Friends and Community

FRIENDS HELP. WHETHER they are few or plentiful, close or casual, they play an important role in coping with the loss of a child, especially in those early moments when life seems to be crashing down around us.

When Christopher was killed the response from our friends was immediate and caring. We found that the circle of those who cared about us was much larger than we could have imagined. In the small village where we live, word of tragedy travels quickly. And so it was that some of our closest friends arrived even before the ambulance had left our driveway. Even the family doctor raced to our home in a patient's car he had urgently commandeered in his effort to provide whatever help to Christopher that he could.

The warm wave of people who came to us in those first days following the accident helped to soften the blow from which we found ourselves reeling. They brought us food and stayed with us until we went to bed late at night. When we got up in the morning, they were there with coffee and breakfast. They surrounded us with support and caring and temporarily filled in the frightening, confusing void that death leaves in its wake.

While these friends gave us room to be alone when we needed it, they also were there to insure that we were not alone when solitude would have overpowered us. At those times their mere presence was a comfort in itself. They gave us an outlet for our heartache as well as the needed shoulder to cry on. It was not so much the words they *spoke* to us—for in the face of death there are no magic words to take away the pain—it was instead the grieving words to which they *listened*. And as they listened, they cried with us . . . for Christopher, for our family, for themselves, and for the fragile hold that we humans have on life.

Yet some friends will feel compelled to act and relieve the mourning parents of any burdens that may face them. This is a sensitive area, and one where it is easy to go too far. I know of a situation in which something as seemingly innocent as polishing the dead child's shoes hurt a parent very much. The mother who told me of this incident explained that a well-meaning relative took the shoes and cleaned them for the burial. The mother lamented, "My daughter's shoes were never polished. She always scuffed them up. The shiny shoes just weren't her." The problem could have been avoided if the relative had simply asked the mother if she wanted the shoes to be polished.

Another mother told me of a painful incident during a visit with a neighbor shortly after her toddler's death. The neighbor's daughter, who had been a playmate of the dead child, came into the room. The neighbor asked the mother if she would like to hold her. The last thing the bereaved mother wanted to do was to hold another child.

In both of these instances, the relative and the neighbor were acting out of love and concern. Their actions weren't "wrong," but they *were* painful. As a friend you can't get inside the heads of the grieving. If you have also lost a child you may come much closer than most, but even then each parent's experience and needs are unique.

So don't be surprised if the grieving fall apart over some relatively minor incident—over something you or someone else says or does with the best of intentions. Try to be understanding; stick with them through their ups and downs. Weigh their visible responses to your attempts to help. Usually their emotions are so near the surface you will be able to read them like an open book. Ask the parents before you do anything that might tamper with their memories of their child.

Perhaps one of the best examples of just how supportive friends can be in these times of loss was demonstrated by our neighbors. We heat our home with wood, as do many of those who live in our small town. Preparing the winter's supply of firewood is a mammoth undertaking, since our heating season begins as early as September and continues well into May.

At the time of Christopher's death, I had just bought an eight-cord load of wood in what we call "log length"—that is, logs about fifteen feet long. The wood had been delivered just a few days before my cancer was discovered. After my surgery I knew I would be physically unable to cut it for the coming winter. Beyond the physical problem I faced, I was now confronted with the mental demotivation that so often immobilizes those who have experienced a tragedy. As far as I was concerned, the wood could just sit and rot while we used the more expensive alternative, fuel oil, in the cold months facing us.

As we drove into our driveway after Christopher's burial in Ohio, I noticed that the huge pile of logs that had been at the edge of our yard was gone. My first thought was that they had been stolen (which would have been no easy task, since the logs were so large and heavy). Parking the car, I walked around to the back of our house and found eight cords of freshly cut firewood stacked in perfect piles, already drying for the coming winter. In our mailbox was an envelope with some beautiful photographs of all the neighbors cutting and stacking the wood. The pictures were accompanied by a simple, four-word note that said all that could be said—"We love you Brambletts!" I know some of the neighbors had not spoken for months, but our tragedy pulled them together, if only for a day, to give unselfishly to us the help we needed. The note and the photographs were worth more to us than all the firewood in Vermont. Our neighbors' gesture will never be forgotten.

But some of the gestures of support Mairi and I appreciated most were often the least dramatic or the least visible. Let me list a few:

- The local restaurateur who brought an enormous platter of food to our house on the day after the accident and slipped away with no recognition at the time

- The ministers who conducted Christopher's funeral service with such caring and love and who patiently worked with Mairi and I when it seemed so impossible to plan anything, much less a funeral

- The dear friend who read the eulogy at our local funeral service when I was unable to do so

- The young woman who sang the special songs we requested at the funeral even though she really didn't know our family

- My two brothers-in-law, who drove two hours each way to meet Christopher's body at the Pittsburgh airport rather than leaving it to strangers

- The father of a child killed in a house fire the year before Christopher's death who left a note on my desk the day I returned to work. The ten-word note meant so much to me as I tried to rejoin the world—"Just to let you know I'm thinking of you today"

- A former coworker who phones me on Christopher's birthday and the anniversary of his death to "touch base"

- The neighbor who brings us a special Christmas ornament each year on Christopher's birthday

These all are special memories for me. At the beginning, just after the death, the primary gift you can give as a friend is, simply, support. In the longer term, the gift is remembrance. I continue to be amazed by the number of our friends who remember us with a card, a letter, a phone call, or visit on Christopher's birthday or the anniversary of his death.

While there is no master plan for serving the needs of the bereaved, if I had to offer advice on what *not* to do, I would suggest the following:

- Don't go visit out of curiosity.

- Don't give them advice on how they should feel.

- Don't tell them not to cry. Encourage them to show their emotions. Better yet, cry with them.

- Don't try to rush their grieving process. It will take months or years before they return to what you think of as "their old selves." (Remember, this may never be completely accomplished.)

- Don't expect them to always respond to your gestures of kindness and support with enthusiasm or overt appreciation. They are shaken to the depths of their souls, and their reactions may not reflect their true appreciation.

- Don't push religion or secular cures for their pain. What they need, they will seek. Only offer your viewpoint in these areas if they seem receptive.

- Don't abandon them because they are difficult to be around. Be patient with their moodiness, their lack of zeal for life.

- Don't complain about minor problems in your life when you do spend time with them.

- Don't think because they have other children things should be better.

- Don't think that encouraging them to have another child will resolve their pain. You cannot replace a dead child.

Spend your energy on the "do's," remember the "don'ts." Most of all, be available. Always be willing to hear the death story one more time—not just during the first months but years later.

*　　　*　　　*

When we take the support of friends and multiply it, it becomes *community*. Our community folded its arms around us from the beginning, perhaps most demonstratively at the funeral.

Christopher's service turned out to be a beautiful tribute of love from a caring community. This outpouring of support was not only for us; it was also for the man who had run over Christopher, and it was for the community itself. Together we all shared the grief and the love that came from Christopher's life and death. How reassuring it was to us to know that our choice to live in this small Vermont town was based on the very values that were now being proven so clearly through action.

Many of you who have lost a child may have faced the near-empty church that I feared so much. Let me assure you that I do not see the size of the church attendance as some sort of measure of how well accepted you or your child may have been in your community. I feel it is more accurately a reflection of the character of the community. Some are warm and loving; others are geared toward a sort of anonymity that isolates its members from sharing joy or grief. These more impersonal communities are increasingly common. They offer a form of privacy valued by many, and they ask nothing more than superficial involvement from those who live there. Unfortunately they usually give back no more than they ask.

My family and I are fortunate to live in a community rare in today's urban/suburban society, one in which the commitment for caring has been proven to us over and over again—most especially after Christopher's death. For those who live in communities that are less tightly knit, draw your strength and support from friends and family. It's not the number of people who grieve with us that is important; it is the sincerity of those who join us in our grief. If it is only one or two who truly cares, then that is enough. Where there is no one to grieve with you, the support groups mentioned in the chapter on reaching out to others (Chapter 13) can help to fill the void.

*   *   *

Regardless of what form our support network may take, we may still encounter uncomfortable moments with those we count as friends. Just a month or so after our return from Christopher's funeral in Ohio, our closest friends arranged an informal get-together for dinner. The dinner was to celebrate the fortieth birthday of one of the wives in the group. Most of those attending had participated in the cutting of our firewood for the coming winter, and we had not been with them collectively since before our difficult trip to Ohio. For Mairi and me, it was the first social outing since Christopher's death.

I was apprehensive about the evening, and as the night wore on I found that I felt like some being from another planet. Observing our friends, I saw laughter and smiles along with other indications they were fully enjoying themselves. Meanwhile, I could only focus on the fact that the last time we were at this particular friend's house, Christopher had been with us. On that night, just a few months before, he had played with the host's daughter, who was only a month older than him. Now I saw her again, this time alone, playing with the same toys she had shared with Christopher such a short time ago.

In my self-imposed isolation, I realized how far I was from these friends at this particular time. Just five weeks earlier they had mourned with us in the intense moments following Christopher's accident. While they had been truly hurt by Christopher's death, unlike us they had returned to their normal lives again in scarcely more than a month. For them, the worst was over. Life was moving ahead.

Their recovery was in no way inappropriate. It wasn't that I wanted them to be as somber as we were, but the party atmosphere accentuated how much deeper our hurt was compared to theirs. As I watched them, I felt absolutely isolated.

Mairi and I would not begin to heal significantly for a considerable time to come. And so on this first social evening I saw the distance between our friends and us widen; I realized just where we were and where they were in dealing with Christopher's death. Attempts were made during the course of the party to draw Mairi and me into the pleasantries, but we just weren't ready. I stonewalled every effort to start a conversation, not to be unfriendly or unkind, but because I was so very empty on the inside. I found myself most affronted by the small talk, trivial topics that to me were so frivolous, so unimportant. I remember thinking, "How can I ever enjoy anything again the same way they seem to be enjoying this evening?" Quite frankly I thought I never would.

While the first step in rejoining society may be very painful, it is essential that it occur as soon as possible—hopefully in the early stages of the healing process. It is a step that needs to be taken as soon as you are capable of enduring the few hours such an occasion may entail. And I do mean enduring, for you may find that, despite your love for those you share this time with, it can be extremely taxing to your shaken emotions.

Mairi found it difficult even to go to the grocery store. She felt as if the other people in the store were quietly exchanging comments as they wondered, "Is she the one whose little boy was killed by the garbage truck?" This feeling was not simply paranoia on Mairi's part; exchanges like that do occur. They are a normal manifestation of human curiosity and concern. They occur in all those public places where we come together in our communities—our grocery stores, our churches—those places where we encounter each other, including the grieving, for the first time following some major life event. For the most part these exchanges reflect genuine sympathy on the part of those who participate in them, but for the grieving, the feeling of being on display—of being the focal point of attention—is extremely distressing.

I don't believe there is any easy way around the discomfort of these times—of being in public places when we really don't want to be or of attending the first get-together with friends. I would suggest that one way to reduce some of the discomfort for a grieving parent at these awkward moments is simply to offer a short, personal condolence to them rather than subjecting them to distant stares or downturned eyes. There will be tears, perhaps, in response to your expression of concern, but there will also be gratitude. Something as simple as "We've been thinking about you" is all that's needed. You will feel better for your effort and so will they.

The important thing for parents is that they take these first steps back toward rejoining the mainstream of life—even though it hurts and makes them uncomfortable. In doing so they put the first encounters behind them. Like the rungs on a ladder, each new step moves them up and away from the sometimes crippling grip of their grief.

And so our friends play an essential role in our healing and coping process. In the early stages of grief, they may help with our physical, emotional, and logistical needs. As we move further into the grieving process, they can continue to support us with deeper love and caring. Some will stand up to the test. Those who do will be friends forever.

We rise by raising others—and he who stoops above
the fallen, stands erect.
R.G. INGERSOLL, *Tribute to Roscoe Conkling*

CHAPTER 13

Reaching Out to Others

THE DEATH OF each child is unique, eliciting a seemingly limitless variety of responses in those left behind. Yet much of this experience is universal. The shared experience of the loss of a child can create a special bond among parents who otherwise may be complete strangers to one another. In time, many of those parents become "well" enough to reach out to others who have suffered a similar loss.

We were blessed to have one such intimate stranger reach out to us in our grief during the first month after Christopher's death. As we opened the sympathy cards marked with familiar return addresses, we came to an envelope postmarked from a town where we had no friends or relatives. The note inside was written from a mother named Kathy whose child had died in a house fire the year before. He had been the same age as Christopher. She shared with us her understanding of our pain as well as the encouragement that time would help to ease our hurt. It was the first time since her son's death that she had reached out directly to anyone. Mairi and I were deeply moved by her caring gesture, and we called to invite her and her husband, Roger, to our home—they lived only thirty miles away.

Our first meeting was extremely emotional, but the communion that took place was beneficial not only for us but for the other couple as well. After four years we continue to keep in touch and to share our feelings and experiences when the need is there. I often see Roger on the streets of the town where we both work. We share our thoughts on how we are doing, how our families are getting along. Mairi and Kathy try to get together for a special Christmas lunch each year. Perhaps our greatest gift to each other is our bond as survivors of the loss of a child. That, in itself, seems to be enough, regardless of the frequency of our contact.

This action of "reaching out" can be a very positive experience for grieving parents—both for those who reach out as well as those who receive. As I began to heal, I found I could write brief notes to parents who were at an earlier stage of grief than I, offering them the hope that the experience does get easier with time and encouraging them to accept the differences that would likely surface between husband and wife in their ongoing attempt to deal with their child's death. Though I never wrote with the expectation of receiving a response, often one would arrive. Occasionally a parent would tuck a picture of his child into an envelope with a letter. Several times Mairi and I received telephone calls. Each response expressed gratitude for the opportunity to share the pain with someone who could truly understand.

While my primary motivation in writing to other grieving parents was to tell them of the healing that comes with time, I found sharing my thoughts with others served as therapy for me as well. As I grew in my faith, I read and reread 2 Corinthians 1:3–4, which calls us to share the comfort we find when we are afflicted. "Praise be to the God and Father of our Lord Jesus Christ, the Father of compassion and the God of all comfort, who comforts us in all our troubles, so that we can comfort those in any trouble with the comfort we ourselves have received from God." I found that the message in this two-thousand-year-old scripture contained such truth in the way it now applied to my life. I am convinced that the comfort which comes to us in our times of grief is given by God as a gift to be shared with others who are similarly touched by pain.

One of the most touching episodes of "reaching out" occurred when we received a letter from a mother who lost two children in an automobile accident in New York State only a month before Christopher's death. The children were in their twenties—and one was the identical twin of one of the mother's remaining children. She had heard of Christopher's death from my wife's sister, who worked with her, and despite the immensity of her own loss, she was able to reach out to us—to help us in our time of need. With her letter she sent a small book entitled *I Will Not Leave You Desolate* by Martha Hickman (printed by the Upper Room, Nashville, Tennessee). The book contained a beautiful and helpful discussion of the grieving and healing process the author had gone through after her teenage daughter was killed in an accident.

After reading the book, I called the woman who had sent it to us and found that she kept a supply of the books on hand, to send to grieving parents whose path somehow crossed hers. Her caring gesture has been multiplied, for Mairi and I now do the same.

A number of months after this first telephone contact, I learned that two children from a Vermont family were killed in a similar automobile accident. One of the victims also was a twin. While I could have written to the grieving parents myself, I realized that no one could share their pain better than our new friend in New York. And so I called her again, asking if she would write our fellow Vermonters. She did write, and I am sure her reaching out provided as much comfort as we human beings can provide to each other in such a loss.

The process of reaching out can truly take remarkable turns and transcend such seemingly insurmountable barriers as cultural and social differences. Let me share with you a particularly interesting story. A few months after Christopher's death, I was attending a conference in Washington, D.C. As the conference ended, I loaded my car and started the long drive back to Vermont. For some reason I picked a less direct route for my journey than I might have normally taken. After several hours I found myself in the heart of Amish country. As I drove down the state highway an upcoming road sign caught my eye: Kutztown. My college roommate Tom Martin was from Kutztown.

The instant I saw the exit sign, a powerful feeling rushed over me. I felt that if I were to exit, I would find my old roommate at his parents' home. I dismissed this thought with some difficulty, for I knew that Tom now lived in New Jersey with his wife and young daughter.

I drove nine miles more fighting an inexplicable urge to turn around and go back. As there was no basis for the belief about my roommate, I sought to dismiss it. But when I reached the next exit, I impulsively drove back toward Kutztown.

I had been alone all week at a hotel in Washington while I attended the conference. I had missed my family immensely. Christopher had been dead only three months, and I still found it very difficult to be away from home. I knew very little about the Amish and Mennonites who made this area their home, but I did know that they were very family-centered, and, after a week alone, I needed family. Perhaps I could spend the night with an Amish or Mennonite family—surely there would be a boardinghouse of some sort run by these people. I certainly could stay with Tom's family, but there would be no children there, and I felt I needed that type of contact.

In Kutztown, I began to search for a place to stay. When I saw a young woman approaching my car on a bicycle, I rolled down my window and explained that I was looking for an Amish or Mennonite boardinghouse. The woman smiled, summing me up as a tourist as she said, "Those folks don't take people in. Their whole 'thing' is keeping separate from outsiders."

I persisted and asked if she knew any of these people personally. She said her neighbors were Old Order Mennonites—horse-and-buggy types. Questioning her further, I learned that the husband and wife were about my age and that they had a large number of children. Her disbelief grew as I told her that if she would give me directions to their farm, I would ask them about spending the night.

After a skeptical comment ("They won't let you stay with them") she gave me the directions. As an afterthought I asked, "Do you happen to know the Martins?" If this woman had been raised in Kutztown, perhaps she knew Tom's family.

She laughed and said there were lots of Martins in Kutztown. She did, however, know two families—one whose father was a dentist, another in the engineering business. I told her that the Martins I knew were in engineering.

The young woman looked surprised. "Their daughter is my best friend!" I then explained that their son had been my roommate in college. Her reply matched my thoughts. "What a coincidence!"

Following the directions she had given me, I made my way to the outskirts of Kutztown and pulled into the driveway that bordered a two-hundred-year-old stone farmhouse. Some young Mennonite children were sitting quietly at a vegetable stand by the driveway, and I asked them where their father was. They pointed to the barn—never speaking a word.

It was a steamy hot June day, and as I walked toward the barn sweat beaded up on my forehead—both from the heat and from the mild anxiety I was beginning to feel about approaching a total stranger whose culture was years apart from my own to ask for a place to stay for the night.

Before I could dwell on my discomfort, I saw the Mennonite farmer emerge from the barn and begin walking toward me. He had seen me pull in and met me about halfway up the curving driveway.

He spoke first. "Hello, my name is Levi Stoltzfus. What can I do for you?"

A large lump rose in my constricting throat as I said to him, "My name is John Bramblett, and I was wondering if I could spend the night with you and your family tonight." Had I really said this? How would I react if someone I didn't know pulled into my driveway with the same question? I felt a bit queasy and foolish as I wondered what he must be thinking.

Without showing any surprise, Levi questioned, "Why do you want to do that?"

"Because I believe it is intended to be." I then explained the circumstances that had led me to his farm. He seemed open to the explanation, and as our conversation continued I grew more comfortable. I told him that I knew a respectable family in Kutztown whom he could call to verify my credibility. "The man's name is Bill Martin," I told him. Bill was Tom's father.

For the first time since our conversation had ensued, I saw a reaction from Levi. My words seemed to knock him back a few inches.

"You know Bill Martin?" he asked with obvious surprise in his voice.

"Yes I do," I explained. "His son was my roommate in college."

The farmer then offered the reason for his surprised reaction. "When I saw you pull in the driveway in your car, I thought you *were* Bill Martin. He has a car just like yours!" Mr. Martin, it seems, was a regular customer at the farm and had become friends with Levi and his family.

Levi shook his head and, smiling, said he didn't need any additional assurances, that I could stay for the night. He wouldn't need any verification, but I was welcome to use his telephone to call the Martins to say hello. We walked to the house together where I phoned the Martins. Bill was quite surprised to hear from me and even more surprised to learn that I was in Kutztown and staying at Levi's farm. "How did you arrange that?" he questioned.

I offered an abbreviated explanation of the day's events and followed with a question about Tom. "How has Tom been?"

It was my turn for a shock as Bill said, " Why don't you ask him, he's right here!" While I waited for Tom to come to the phone, I reflected on the impulses and the outcomes of this most unusual day. Those impulses had led me to a series of total strangers—strangers who were intimately connected with people who were my friends. Now, I would talk to Tom who, by all rights, should have been at his home in New Jersey. My intuitions were now being confirmed. Tom was in Kutztown.

Tom shared my amazement. He had been home for two weeks and was leaving before dawn the next day. Had I waited to call him our paths would not have crossed. He and his father drove out to the farm, and we had a wonderful visit around the kitchen table of my newly found Mennonite friends. After the Martins left, Levi, his wife, and I sat and talked until past midnight about their way of life and mine.

Our visit together had been exceptionally meaningful for both me and Levi and his wife, and as I walked out to my car the next morning we exchanged addresses so we could correspond in the future. When I asked why they had decided to take me in, Levi quoted a verse from the Bible, "Be not forgetful to entertain strangers: for thereby some have entertained angels unawares." I suggested I was no angel. Levi's reply made me pause, "No, probably not, but you may be travelling with one." I, of course, thought of Christopher.

About six weeks after this visit I received a letter from my new friends in Pennsylvania. The letter contained some sad and, at the same time, ironic news. A short time after my visit, a tragedy occurred in the family of one of their cousins. The cousin's two-year-old son was killed in an accident involving a large truck, much in the same way that Christopher had been killed. I found other amazing parallels between that family and ours. There were only three days, difference between the ages of Christopher and their son. Both boys were run over in full view of their mothers. This Mennonite family had two boys about the same ages as Brian and John, and their youngest daughter was only three weeks older than Meghan.

We wrote to the grieving parents and shared our feelings with them. They in turn wrote to us, and as our correspondence continued, we saw that, despite the fact that they traveled by horse and buggy and lived without television and radio, the pain of the death of our children drew us together. A year after our correspondence began, I met our new friends for the first time. A few months later, Mairi, Meghan, and I stayed with them for a wonderful three-day visit on their Lancaster County farm. We now visit them twice a year, sharing love that is not bound by the differences in the way we dress or live.

We have helped each other despite the differences in our cultural circumstances, proving the point that shared suffering and shared comfort are common denominators that can melt away our outward differences. Those who make the effort to reach out become part of a beneficial healing process.

There are other ways to reach out as well. It need not be limited to other grieving parents but may extend to anyone who has experienced pain in its varying facets.

About six months after Christopher was killed, I surveyed my personal schedule and found a wasted hour in my weekly routine. On Tuesday nights I had a Rotary meeting at 6:30. My usual pattern was to finish work at 4:30, drive directly to the Rotary meeting, and sit in the lounge for an hour or so, drinking soda and eating the complimentary peanuts at the restaurant where we met. There really wasn't enough time to go home before the meeting, yet the hour in the lounge was a waste of time.

I began to review the ways in which I could best use that hour. The thought crossed my mind that when Christopher was hospitalized with his viral croup, I saw other children whose parents could not be with them—either because of distance, obligations, or, more sadly, by choice. I decided to see if my extra hour could be used more constructively at the nearby medical center.

I became an hour-a-week volunteer on the pediatrics ward. I found that my experience with cancer and with losing Christopher made it possible to offer support to parents who were dealing with sick and sometimes dying children.

My volunteer work also allowed me to meet others who were suffering in various ways—among them a young man who had just become a paraplegic in an accident. I spoke first with the man's distraught mother. She explained that not only was she herself still trying to cope with the current tragedy but that her son's comments hinted that he was thinking of suicide. Other people were present when I first went to see him. Just before we left, the paralyzed man said he could not imagine living like this forever; he then added, ''At least I can still use my hands.'' It seemed obvious he was alluding to suicide.

I waited behind as everyone else left the room. Then, leaning very close to him, I whispered, ''I can't put myself in your place right now; I can't imagine what faces you; but I can tell you that there was a time not long ago when life seemed to mean nothing to me either. You see, I was diagnosed with cancer, and three weeks later my two-year-old son was run over and killed as my wife watched helplessly. I reached the point where I didn't care if I lived or died. But I found, as I hope you will, that there were people who still needed me and loved me, and slowly I regained my own love of life.''

Tears welled up in his eyes as they did in mine. As I left, he thanked me for sharing my pain and my hope. He has survived, and so have I.

Some parents may find they are more able to give or receive support from organized grief-support groups, many of them established specifically for parents who have lost children. They are an excellent resource for those who are more comfortable with a group approach to discussing their feelings. Quite often their format offers the opportunity just to sit quietly, listening to others express their grief, or to share your own feelings and thoughts with those around you as and when you choose.

Generally these support groups can be located through neighborhood churches. Though they may meet at a church, they tend to be nondenominational. Many are organized around secular themes and activities and only meet in churches because the space is provided to them at no cost.

At the national level there are a number of organizations that may be of help. Perhaps the best known is The Compassionate Friends, which has chapters in almost every state. The address of their headquarters is:

The Compassionate Friends
National Headquarters
P.O. Box 3696
Oak Brook, Illinois 60522-3696

A group specifically established for parents of children who have been murdered is Parents of Murdered Children, headquartered in Cincinnati, Ohio. It, too, has a number of chapters, primarily in large metropolitan areas of the country. The address is:

Parents of Murdered Children, Inc.
100 East 8th Street
Cincinnati, Ohio 45202

There is also a national support organization for parents of children who have cancer or have died from it:

Candlelighters Foundation
1312 18th Street, N.W.
Washington, D.C. 20036

Parents who have lost a child or infant through an unexplained death, often known as Sudden Infant Death Syndrome (SIDS) or crib death, can contact this national organization:

National Sudden Infant Death Syndrome (SIDS) Foundation
10500 Little Patuxent Parkway
Suite 420
Columbia, Maryland 21044
1-800-638-7437

The most important thing to remember is that, regardless of the form it takes, the effort of reaching out speeds the healing process for both those who give and those who receive.

Do not seek death. Death will find you. But seek the
road which makes death a fulfillment.
DAG HAMMARSKJÖLD, *Markings*

CHAPTER 14

Some Afterthoughts About Death

CHRISTOPHER'S UNTIMELY DEATH forced me to think
deeply about death in general. Of course, we all know about
death and its relationship to us as individuals. It is the unwelcome intruder that visits each of us once, and only once, in a
lifetime. It robs our bodies of life, leaving a cold, empty shell
behind for those who grieve. Or it leaves us, the living, behind,
taking someone we love instead.

Death is an awful thing to see. Its remnants are often ugly.
Violent death shocks us with bloodied, violated bodies that
leave us cringing as we speculate on the agony that the person
may have endured before his death.

Even when death comes without violence its visit is usually
unwelcome, although sometimes, ironically death becomes a
blessing after an extended illness. In any case, whether it is
sudden or follows a long illness, we, the survivors, mourn the
loss while we give up the body. At the same time we try
desperately to hold onto the memories of the one we've lost.

Death moves ever closer toward us with each passing moment, ultimately finding each of us in these or a thousand other
ways. Consider the sobering thought that you are closer to it

now than you were when you started reading this paragraph.

Although we normally shy away from thoughts such as these, sadly, it is our very reluctance to look at the face of death until it directly confronts us that causes us so much difficulty when it finally does threaten.

Looking back across the years, I recall my first encounter with death: the death of my cat. I was only eight years old. The cat, cornered in the basement of our house, was torn to shreds by several neighborhood dogs. The incident occurred while I was away from home, and my parents decided to try to protect me from the pain of this first loss by not telling me what had happened. When I returned home later that evening, my parents said nothing as I repeatedly called for my cat. But as the hours passed and they watched me make trip after trip to the back door, they knew they could no longer hide the truth from me.

My mother told me in a faltering voice that my cat would not be answering my call. When I asked why, she gently explained that my cat was dead. My reaction was one of distress and of anger. Anger at my parents for not telling me what had happened sooner and anger at the dogs for stealing my cat from me. Anger was followed by denial. These classic grief reactions fit the way we respond to death at any age.

I said that my cat couldn't be dead. I demanded, "Show me where it was killed" so that I could believe it. In the basement bits of fur—fur I had stroked so lovingly, so often—were scattered about the cold dirt floor. I then asked to see the body. That was not possible as the cat had been buried already, so they showed me the grave. As I stood there by the small mound of red Georgia dirt, I cried and I grew angrier. Not only was my cat dead, but all I had left now to document this first encounter with death was this small grave, a few bits of fur, and my aching memories.

My anger turned to action. I ran to my closet and grabbed my BB gun. For what was left of the evening and for the next several days, I hunted unsuccessfully for the killer dogs, determined to repay them for the hurt they had brought into my life. I never found the dogs. My parents got me another cat.

Life wasn't the same for a while, but eventually I recovered.

My parents' intentions had been good. This was the first death experience we were to go through together. They knew about death. I did not. They wanted to shield me from the pain, but they could not shield me and still honor the truth. In the end they opted, correctly, for the truth.

As I discussed in "Brothers and Sister," echoes of this same desire to protect my own children from pain entered into my thoughts at the time of Christopher's death. What I learned was that we really cannot protect. Our surviving children must experience the pain—must go *through* it, not around it—to get to the other side.

After my cat's death, my next encounter with death was when my grandmother died five years later, when I was thirteen. She suffered a major stroke, lingering in a terrible, debilitated state for a period of weeks. Since she and I were very close, her condition was incredibly upsetting. It hurt me to see her unable to communicate with me. It hurt to see her unable to move. And as the days crept by and she failed to improve, it seemed she would be like this forever.

A few weeks after the stroke my father tiptoed into my room in the early morning. He gently woke me, and in the darkness that surrounded us, he told me Granny had died. After asking when it had happened, I told him I wanted to go back to sleep. Granny was gone. What did it really mean? Had she seen the room slip away? Did she let go and say this isn't so bad after all?

The thing that bothered me most about my grandmother's death was that, as much as I loved her, I couldn't cry. This was just like Meghan's experience almost thirty years later when Christopher was killed. I felt tremendous guilt as a result of my inability to show my emotions. Although everyone around me was openly grieving, I was unable to express my sorrow.

Prior to the funeral, my grandmother's body and casket were kept at my Aunt Abbie's house rather than at a funeral home. (This was an accepted practice in the South at that time.) It was strange but also comforting to see Granny's body lying in the

old parlor where our family had gathered so often to celebrate
the joys of life with her. Relatives and family came and went
during the day, and the immediate family stayed late into the
night. I sat and stared at her open casket for hours, sometimes
alone, sometimes as part of a larger group. My feelings were
an uncomfortable mix of sadness and curiosity. What was it
like to be dead? What was it like at the far end of that long,
dark tunnel when you let go and don't come back? How long
was the forever that would follow? Why do our bodies fail and
die?

I had a strong desire to touch my dead grandmother, perhaps
to answer the unspoken question tumbling around in my young
mind, "How does a dead body feel?" My twelve-year-old
cousin Mary Ann and I discussed this preoccupation at length.
She felt the same curiosity. Neither of us were sure whether our
feelings were normal.

When Mary Ann's mother came into room, she seemed to
sense our mood and asked if we were all right. We explained
our desire to touch Granny. I think both Mary Ann and I were
surprised when her mother told us that our feelings were perfectly normal, and that she would stand with us while we held
Granny's hand. With her by our sides, we walked to the casket
and touched my grandmother's hand. It was a good thing to do.
It told me a lot about death.

I can still feel the cold, hard flesh. The thing that struck me
most was that her hand was colder than the temperature of the
room. It was as if not only the warmth of life had been drained,
but that unnatural cold had somehow been substituted in its
place. It made death real for me. Not pleasant. Not understand-
able. But real.

After Christopher was killed and I touched him in the casket
the first time, that same coldness was there. His hands had been
deceptively warm earlier that day in our driveway, hinting of
life. They fed my desire to deny the obvious. A few hours later
at the funeral home his hands were just like my grandmother's
hand had been so long ago. For both the old and the young who
leave us, this is what death is like: still, rigid, cold.

Over the thirty years since my grandmother's death, I have

experienced the death of loved ones many more times. In 1985, when I was diagnosed with a potentially terminal case of cancer, I was suddenly forced to focus on my own eventual death. In the days just following my diagnosis, I found that I began to view the actions of others from the perspective of "the dying patient," and that my attitude toward them changed. When my wife's thoughts about my cancer turned to questions of what she and the kids would do if I were to die, I saw her as remarkably selfish. I was the one facing death, and yet she seemed more concerned about her own well-being than what might lie ahead for me. Of course, I too, was concerned for my family, but it was my own selfishness, my lack of preparedness for and my fear of death, that caused me to react to her in this way. I was unable to appreciate how vulnerable she felt about the possibility of losing me as her companion and provider.

As I have discussed, I made little or no progress in facing the prospect of my own death in the three short weeks following my diagnosis—and on April 17, 1985, I most certainly wasn't ready when death struck so quickly and took my youngest child. In an instant Christopher moved from his innocent play in the security of my sun-soaked yard to the other side of death's impenetrable, mysterious door. He was gone before my assaulted senses could even begin to assimilate what was happening. Christopher's death forced me to face more directly the possibility of my own death, but more importantly, the issue of death in general.

The fact itself is simple: we are *all* terminal—healthy or sick, young or old, rich or poor. We all must and will die.

The only unanswerable and temporal question that remains for us is when and how our lives will end. And although death is the one thing we can be absolutely certain of, almost all of us live life avoiding the issues surrounding it until they face us head-on.

We *should* deal with the issues of death before a crisis of some sort intervenes, although we should not spend our time in an unhealthy preoccupation with death. Yet we will find death's confrontations easier to face if we are prepared.

How do we prepare and what do we learn as we face the

issue of death? Perhaps its ultimate lesson is that we can't hold onto "things"—not just the "things" we spend so much of life accumulating, but life itself—our own life, that of our spouse's, our parent's . . . or even our children's. While we may live our lives in an attempt to avoid the very idea that death can make its entry into our protected worlds, it ultimately will. In our naivete we almost convince ourselves that if we don't think about it, we will elude it.

At some point we *will* be confronted with a terminal diagnosis, a parent's or a spouse's death, or the loss of a child. Suddenly we will find ourselves swirling helplessly in deep, dark water, in the midst of the most difficult experience life has to offer—and most of us will be unprepared for it. Death will have closed, or will be about to close, a door that seems impossible to open. But there is a key to the door.

The key is faith.

God often visits us, but most of the time we are not home.
JOSEPH ROUX, *Meditations of a Parish Priest*

CHAPTER 15

Thoughts on Faith

IF YOU WANT to start a controversy, bring up the subject of "faith" in a group. Discussions of faith inevitably spill over into talk of "religion," of how man institutionalizes the practice of faith. And it is the institutionalization of things—regardless of their nature—that breeds controversy. Countless denominations, sects, cults, and other collections of various types of "believers" have evolved to reveal how differently man institutionalizes his beliefs. Organizing beliefs into dogmas, into rituals, often impersonalizes the basic elemental faith that links man and God. How can man improve on a divine relationship by placing it in the framework of secular rules? While fellowship with other believers is critical to faith, too much structure may kill it.

For many of us, raising the question of faith at all sets the stage for an overt and possibly unpleasant personal confrontation. What we choose to believe is one of the most sensitive matters in our world today. It is something we consider our own business unless we mutually agree to share it with someone else. The confrontation becomes more uncomfortable when we are facing one of life's other difficult issues and someone comes along offering their religion as the answer to all of our problems.

Yet when we have lost a child or someone else we love it seems that the question of what we believe or don't believe is unavoidable. If no one else asks us the question, surely we must ask it of ourselves. If we are truly to move toward resolution of the death within the context of the rest of our lives, we must arrive at some answer to that question.

In *Beyond Endurance: When a Child Dies*, Dr. Knapp reports on his extensive clinical study of parents who have lost children. One finding of particular significance was that the vast majority of the 155 parents he interviewed turned to faith as a source of comfort for their hurt. Many of these grieving parents had professed no faith before the death of their child. For some the spiritual awakening was immediate; for others it was more gradual. And many of those who turned to faith seemed to find a genuine source of strength for coping with their loss.

Dr. Knapp's book is just one of many I have read in the time since my son's death. Although Dr. Knapp has never lost a child himself, I have also read books by parents who *have* lost children. One notable characteristic these books have in common is their failure to address the issue of faith in any depth. Important as faith can be to coping with loss, it is given only passing attention in these works—perhaps because our different religions provide controversy and division more than comfort. When we are trying to help others who are in pain, our goal is certainly not to alienate them on any issue but to unite with them. Ironically those books that do address faith often paint a picture of a rather helpless God who stands to one side, unable to do anything but watch as tragedy after tragedy crushes those He has created.

In my own effort to relate my experience in losing Christopher, I deliberately saved the discussion of faith for last. I place it last not because I find it was the least important element in resolving my grief. Placing this discussion at the end of my story allows you first to consider the more secular elements surrounding Christopher's death and my effort to cope with them without confronting you with the more ambiguous problems connected with the mysteries of faith as well. This approach actually parallels my own experience: first I had to work through the physical issues surrounding Christopher's death, and while doing so I moved, ever so slowly, toward a spiritual understanding of my loss.

As we proceed, let me share with you the central role faith came to play in my acceptance of both my son's death and my own illness. I have to emphasize that my faith *grew*; it was not strong at the beginning. So if you have little faith, or none at all, don't be intimidated or put off by the discussion that follows.

Faith offers to us the promise of extending life forever—life not in the form or substance we now know it, but one which has no pain, no tears, no suffering. I learned of this promise through the Christian faith.

Many of you familiar with contemporary Christianity are no doubt saying to yourself, "I've read enough. I know all I need to know about those pushy phonies who call themselves Christians." You've seen the Christian media scandals, with the self-righteous, self-appointed messengers of Christianity whose sole motivation seems to be building empires and bathing themselves in the luxury derived from gullible followers. But before you close the book, I ask you to look beyond the hypocritical, greed-filled things done in the name of Christianity to the true Christianity, one that has brought immeasurable peace to me and my family in the face of Christopher's death and my cancer.

There are people who seem as if they were born to face life's most difficult moments from the unshakable foundation of genuine faith. It is no small miracle to watch these fellow human beings bear life's pain in a non-self-righteous demonstration of inner strength. In difficult times they are able to stand, not devoid of human emotions and tears, but possessed of an outlook based on hope rather than despair. Unfortunately this was not the case for me.

As I knelt over my dead son on that cold April day in 1985, I must confess that my confused faith was unable to provide me with that hope. Despite the fact that I had learned about God and Christ years before, these early teachings had long since been put on hold while I immersed myself in the material world. Self-indulgence became my primary source of pleasure, and I moved away from my Christian path substituting in its place a morally oriented but inadequate form of humanistic religion. All it required was the vague acceptance of a God who was primarily manifested through nature, one who required nothing more of me than the completion of as many good deeds as possible during my time on earth. In my mind these good works would guarantee me a comfortable place in the life beyond this, if, in fact, there truly was one.

Despite these feelings, I still called myself a Christian. I could recite from memory a range of key Bible verses; I knew the story of the Ten Commandments; I could provide you with an accurate historical overview of Christ's life, death, and resurrection; and I felt that church attendance, along with doing "good" things consistent with the "thou shalt nots" found in the Bible were the basis for getting into heaven. I believed in the deity of Christ, but I was hesitant to commit to the fact that He and He alone was "the way, the truth, and the life" and that "no man comes to the Father" except by Him. I felt that this position was simply too narrow and old-fashioned for to-day's progressive world. Lastly I didn't read the Bible very much. It seemed that the heavy dose of scripture and sermon on Sunday morning was more than adequate to meet any religious needs I had.

In retrospect, I was spiritually limited by operating only in the world of the rational mind, the emotions, and the current reality. I followed Christian principles only to the extent that they didn't interfere with my success in, and involvement with, the modern world. Unfortunately, like most others who operate this way, I was poorly equipped to handle life's most difficult moments. In fact, I was no better off in these situations than those who have no belief at all. Tragically, I didn't find this out until life came crashing down all around me. Unlike the non-believer, who has no higher being to address his anger toward, my confused faith seriously questioned the same God I once professed to worship.

As I was confronted with the worst that life can offer, I awoke to how empty my faith had been. This awakening was extremely painful and frightening.

Christopher's death, preceded by my cancer diagnosis, served as a devastating assault on my self-serving, shallow faith. Very quickly and clearly I saw how inadequate my faith truly was. Ironically such major assaults on our fragile humanity actually seem to simplify the issue of faith and its place in our lives. When we are under attack, we can take only one of two very different and divergent paths—either our faith is tested in the light of the new hardship and subsequently survives and grows, or it is destroyed. Even those who profess no faith must look for answers beyond themselves at these difficult times. Perhaps you have heard the old adage that developed during one of the wars: "There are no atheists in foxholes."

My confrontation with faith began that April day in 1985 as I studied Christopher's stilled face—the same sweet face that had smiled at me so many times when I had no smile to return . . . when the weary journey I was on had robbed me of the ability to return in kind the innocent love he extended to me. I knew then there were only two possibilities—either this tragic world was all there was or there was something far greater beyond this life that I did not yet comprehend. In that painful moment I realized I must pursue the answer to this question with all the energy that remained within me.

In these rare moments of extreme pain, we may sense just for an instant that something does lie beyond the mists of this confining physical world in which we live. We may experience a heightened awareness that hints that there is truly more to life and death than our limited senses are capable of perceiving amid the continuous rush of worldly interference. The experience of opening ourselves to this awareness is almost impossible to describe, yet when we sense it, we know with all certainty that it is absolutely real. It was at the moment of

Christopher's death that I had such an experience. I began to push back all interferences—the world around me, the self within me—and I began to search.

As the search for answers continued, I concluded that God had not caused, but he had *allowed*, Christopher's death and my cancer to occur. I began to realize that God seemed to be using them as a means to call me back home—not as a punishment but as a startling confrontation with matters of eternal consequence. He placed the issues of life and death squarely before me, forcing me to focus, as I had never done before, on what I *really* believed. From this new perspective I began to sense that Christopher's death was not the end of his journey but a major transitional point along life's way. If I could believe the precepts of Christianity, Christopher was not dead but was with God. For the first time in my adult life I found myself earnestly seeking to know this God I had so long professed to believe in. As I sought, there seemed to come a response.

Very shortly after the accident my family and I became aware of what seemed to be a remarkable process of interaction between God and us, one where "roadmarks" seemed to be planted to alert us to His presence. It was almost as if God were pulling us close to convey that, despite the pain, everything was all right. At first we thought we were simply suffering from a group bout of wishful thinking and delusion, but as the frequency and intensity of these moments of awareness of God's presence increased, we began to call them "little miracles." Whereas we had initially discounted them as mere coincidence, we came to realize that they seemed to have a purpose. They were there to provide us with comfort as well as to feed our faith. In our newfound openness we began to see things with new eyes.

If you have experienced the awareness of God's presence of which I speak, you know full well that I haven't lost my mind. If you haven't had this experience, let me assure you that my mental health is far better than it has ever been. As difficult as it may be for the rational mind to accept, I now believe God works in supernatural ways and is more than able to interact directly with us in our natural world. All of us are exposed to "little miracles" day after day, but in our rush of activity we often don't have the presence of mind to see them. We simply are not open to them. Those to which we do give fleeting recognition are generally dismissed as mere coincidence.

So how do we achieve this openness? Let me explain how it developed for me. As you read remember that I am an engineer by training. My structured mind has always demanded a tangible cause—a rational, logical explanation—for everything I have encountered. It was this ordered mind that was part of the "interference" standing between me and true spirituality. Beyond this mindset, other things also stood in the way.

We are continually barraged with what we might call the "static of life." Our jobs, outside commitments, the demands of family life, internal stresses and drives, the six o'clock news, and a myriad of other forces all vie for our attention. They usually have it until something so devastating happens that it leaves us absolutely broken. These crushing events then sweep all the interference aside, leaving us open to our most elemental feelings, thoughts, and impressions. Like concentric circles spreading out from the spot where we toss a stone into the water, the interference moves out and away, leaving a smooth, unbroken surface in its wake. In these unusually lucid moments we become sensitized to the spiritual voice within us. With the interference gone, we find we can suddenly see in a spiritual sense as never before. We may recognize that there is a pattern and connectedness to the events in our lives; we may see order where before there appeared to be only chaos.

This new awareness served as a catalyst in my desire to seek God. Some don't need this type of awakening; others claim no interest in seeking God at all. Perhaps I am wrong, but I believe each of us, regardless of what we may profess publicly, would like to believe there is a loving God. But we are uncomfortable with the apparent inconsistencies between the world as it is and the way we would envision it operating under the authority of a loving God.

Often it is only when forces and events beyond our control, like the death of a child, strip us of our worldliness that we may find ourselves yielding, becoming emotionally like little children again. And it is at those times we may find ourselves open to the possibilities of faith—possibilities that were really there all the time, silently waiting beneath the clutter of our busy lives.

Through the catalysts of Christopher's death and my cancer, the layers of worldliness and related interference that had hampered my spiritual vision were peeled away, and I found myself at the very core of my being. I began to truly understand myself, and in this state of heightened sensitivity I also became very aware of life's events being played out around me. Thus I began to see and sense the interconnectedness of many of the events that earlier I would have labelled "coincidence" . . . if I had even noticed a connection at all.

To dispel any of the mystery which may be building at this point, let me share with you two examples of the types of coincidences I am talking about. On the day after Christopher was killed, Mairi and I were meeting at our home with the ministers who would conduct his memorial service the next day. We had chosen one of the few quiet spots in the house that day—our bedroom. As we talked, one of the ministers asked me if there was anything in particular that Christopher really enjoyed that could be mentioned in the service. My immediate thought was of a cuckoo clock I had recently bought for Christopher and Meghan. The clock hung on the wall of their bedroom. It had become the target of many family jokes since it never managed to keep the correct time; Christopher loved the little cuckoo bird so much that I would continually advance the hands to make the bird cuckoo for him. As I told the two ministers how much my son had loved the little bird, there was a soft tapping sound at the window behind me. A look of astonishment came over the faces of the ministers, and they gestured at the window.

Turning quickly, I saw a small bird hovering against the glass. It had not collided with the window but instead was simply fluttering in midair, wings sweeping softly against the windowpane. We were all taken aback by the unusual timing of the bird's appearance. The ministers discussed the apparent connection between the comment I had just made about the

little bird that Christopher loved and the simultaneous arrival of
the real bird at our window. While I was less attuned to the
significance of this event than the two ministers, I sensed that
there was something truly remarkable about the timing of the
incident, something that exceeded my ability to understand it.
The story was retold at the memorial service, leaving many of
my friends with the same feeling that there was more to this
simple coincidence than they could fully comprehend.

A second incident occurred the week after Christopher's
funeral, when we returned to Vermont from Ohio and experienced the emptiness of our home for the first time since our
departure. Within minutes after we had parked the car, I found
myself at the dining room bay window, staring out at a spot in
our yard where Christopher had been playing the day before he
was killed. Tears welled up in my eyes as I remembered how
happy he had been that day. Through the blur of tears I saw an
object lying in the grass. I didn't know what it was, but I
sensed that it did not belong outside.

Quietly I walked out into the yard and around the house.
There on the lawn, underneath the same window where the bird
had appeared, was a small gold-filigree pillbox that had been
passed down through several generations in my wife's family.
It had been her mother's and grandmother's before her.

While I had seen the pillbox many times before I had never
really taken the time to look at it carefully. Now, as I picked
it up from the grass, I saw the porcelain inlay on the lid for the
first time. Etched into the porcelain was a beautiful picture of
a small bird with a note held tightly in its beak flying to the
outstretched hand of a tiny blond cherub angel.

When we had left for Ohio two weeks earlier the pillbox was
in our bedroom. How did it get from our house to the yard? I
asked everyone in my family, but no one had any idea how it
happened. For my family and me, the connection between the
etching and the previous incident involving the bird at our
window carried a message that we simply could not credit to
coincidence.

While these events taken alone could be easily discounted by
even a moderate skeptic, this type of thing continued to occur

frequently, sometimes even more dramatically, in the months that followed. I assure you that my family and I weren't fabricating these events, but their frequency and purposefulness made us increasingly aware of them as time passed.

Perhaps one of the most helpful of these "little miracles" came at the peak of the stress between Mairi and me. It had a major impact in diffusing the tension that had built between us. A few weeks after the funeral—late in the day, just before sunset—the level of stress between Mairi and me had escalated to an unbearable level. Our emotions were boiling, ready to erupt at any moment. Since my parents were still visiting us, I suggested to Mairi that the two of us go outside for a moment rather than subject my parents to what I knew would be a most unpleasant episode between Mairi and me.

I walked out first, with Mairi following. We shut the door and stood facing each other on our breezeway, no more than six feet apart. Not a breath of air stirred in the gathering darkness. In contrast to our combative mood, a pervasive quiet enveloped the breezeway. We stood silently in the dimming twilight, unable to speak the troublesome words that had been spoken so many times before. Finally I broke the standoff.

"Mairi, we can't go on like this. We have to accept the differences in the way we are dealing with all of this."

Mairi said nothing. We had discussed this topic a dozen times before; there was nothing new to say. Her only response was the searching, weary look on her face.

As we stood there in silence, we suddenly heard an unusual sound. There was a soft fluttering followed by the appearance of a small sparrow. It flew *between* us at chest level, quickly disappearing into the darkness. We both thought of the bird at our window the day before the funeral. Now this bird seemed to carry the message, "It's all right to tell the others." Mairi's face softened into a warming smile. I let out a deep sigh, releasing all the tension within me with the exhaled breath. Once again I spoke. "It's okay for us to talk about it, to share it with others."

Her reply was gentle. "I know, it's just so personal."

Standing together now in the growing darkness, we remembered that our boys were planning to attend a dance that night at the local high school. As we turned to go into the garage to pull out the car, Mairi went first and I followed, about two feet behind her. As if to make sure we understood, the sparrow returned and flew between us again—once more at chest height. This time Mairi had her back to the bird, but before I could say anything, she said, "I heard it!"

We are tempted—perhaps even more comfortable—to write these occurrences off as coincidence. But does labelling them with a simple word explain their source, their significance in respect to their benevolent timing and the strengthening of our faith? I think not.

In *New Seeds of Contemplation* Thomas Merton discusses his awareness of the significance of these simple yet special moments in our lives. He writes,

Faith brings together the known and the unknown so that they overlap; or rather, so that we are aware of their overlapping. Actually, our whole life is a mystery of which very little comes to our conscious understanding. But when we accept only what we can consciously rationalize, our life is actually reduced to the most pitiful limitations though we may think quite otherwise. (We have been brought up with the absurd prejudice that only what we can reduce to a rational and conscious formula is really understood and experienced in our life. When we can say what a thing is, or what we are doing, we think we fully grasp and experience it. In point of fact this verbalization—very often it is nothing more than verbalization—tends to cut us off from genuine experience and to obscure our understanding instead of increasing it.)

Faith does not simply account for the unknown, tag it with a theological tag and file it away in a safe place where we do not have to worry about it. This is a falsification of the whole idea of faith. On the contrary, faith incorporates the unknown into our everyday life in a living, dynamic and actual manner. . . .

The fact that these things we sometimes label and casually tuck away occur so perfectly in space and time, that they so often come to us when we truly need them, that they are so obviously reassuring, leads me to the conclusion that they come from a powerful and loving source. Since we humans like labels so much, let me give the source a name—God.

As I read more Christian literature, listened to more personal accounts of similar coincidences, and heard more sermons based on God's supernatural interaction in the lives of not only ancient man but contemporary man as well, my faith grew to the point where I stopped trying to explain things from a scientific or rational standpoint and instead simply began to give God the credit for them as a benevolent spiritual gift. It was not easy to give up the need to satisfy my intellect, but when I did, I found that each new event strengthened my growing faith. Spirituality doesn't demand answers for every question as one's intellect does. It simply asks for an almost childlike openness as the intellect and its limitations yield to the possibility of an Interactive God.

The experiences of my family are not unique. In fact, they appear to be relatively common among grieving parents. Furthermore, I believe that if each of us examined our lives more closely, we would find that these special moments we so often casually dismiss occur to each of us—and more frequently than we take the time to realize.

In my quest to understand the unusual things going on around me, I spoke with other parents who had lost children and found that many had experienced the same sort of occurrences. They, too, had paused along the way and raised the question, "Are we losing our minds, or is this really happening?" Like us, they concluded they were sane; that the experiences were real, not imagined or contrived by wishful thinking. Let me share with you an example of the power of these "little miracles" from another family who lost a child.

I read an article in *Reader's Digest* about a family whose thirteen-year-old son was fatally injured by a teenage drunk driver. In his attempt to accentuate the positive despite the tragedy, the distraught father, Dick, began to speak to high school students throughout the state about teenage alcohol abuse.

The *Digest* article focussed on the content of his speech, interspersing Dick's inner thoughts as he spoke to his audience. One thought seemed out of place until I finished reading the article. Dick kept asking himself, "Should I tell them about the fox?"

Each time this question arose in his mind, he fought it off. "No, if I mention the fox they won't believe me any more, they won't believe the rest of what I have to say." I was puzzled—what did a fox have to do with his message on his family's tragedy, and why would it destroy Dick's credibility with this group of high school students?

As I read on, I discovered the significance of the fox. Two days after Dick's son was killed, the family was gathered in their kitchen when they saw a fox come out of the woods that bordered their backyard. The family was surprised to see the beautiful animal, since they live in a relatively developed area and had never seen a fox in the neighborhood before. They were even more surprised when the creature walked toward the house, right up to the patio, and stood there, staring in the kitchen window. Within a few moments it turned and disappeared into the woods.

Sometime later that same day, Dick's pregnant sister-in-law came by to visit. As they told her about the fox, her face flushed with amazement. The family listened intently as she explained her reaction. When she was considering names for her baby from a baby-name book, she had looked up the name of their own deceased son to see what it had meant. His name, Todd, meant "fox."

The story does not end here. I reflected on the article, thinking how much the event paralleled some of our own experiences, then tucked it away in the corner of my mind. A few weeks later I arranged an appointment with a stone cutter in nearby Barre who had been recommended for Christopher's memorial stone. As I walked into the artisan's noisy shed, I could just make out the silhouette of a solitary man studying a large, uncut piece of granite. He seemed to sense my presence and turned slowly toward me. The fellow was dressed in a pair of baggy trousers, one of those undershirts with the straps at the shoulders, and a newspaper hat like the pirate hats I had made from similar newspapers when I was a small boy. The hat was perforated with scattered holes that had apparently been burned in with a cigarette. (I later learned the holes were for ventilation and also that the newspaper was from Italy.) His appearance disconcerted me; I had expected someone much different.

Surely this could not be the artisan I had selected to create Christopher's memorial. I asked, "Excuse me, but are you Al Fantone?" Hoping he would say no, I was further unsettled by his affirmation that indeed he was Al.

I think Al sensed my surprise at his unusual appearance, and he motioned for me to follow him. He led me around piles of huge granite blocks to a small dust-covered table in the rear of the shed on which lay a notebook filled with pictures and articles about his work. He had pioneered a technique for etching photographic likenesses of people in stone. I turned page after page of photographs of Al's incredible work. He was not just an artisan; he was a master.

Suddenly a picture of a memorial jumped out at me. The picture was of a jet black stone with a portrait etched into its surface—one identical to the photograph of Dick's son that appeared in *Reader's Digest*. I asked Al where he had gotten the picture. He carefully separated the plastic that protected the photo from the dusty air and slid out a copy of *Reader's Digest* article. He told me he had done the stone for the family in the article. And now he would help me with Christopher's as well.

Later that evening I wrote to Dick's family, explaining how I had chanced to meet the man who had done their son's memorial and sharing with them some of the parallels in our own experiences. About a week later the phone rang as I was preparing for bed. It was Dick. He thanked me for my letter, and we spoke (and cried) together for at least a half hour. When I mentioned how reassuring the fox story had been to me after some of our own coincidences, he told me of a second incident. Friends had invited him and his wife to go on an overnight sailing trip with them to help dispel some of their grief for at least one night. While they weren't enthusiastic, they agreed to go. Everyone had retired for the evening and was below decks. Sometime during the night they were awakened by a soft thud from outside the cabin. When they opened the cabin door they saw that a nearby boat had drifted into them. Dick's wife looked up at the mast of the other boat, which was swaying slowly back and forth in the gentle night breeze. There at the top of the mast was a pennant, and the emblem on it was that of a fox!

Once we have climbed over the intellectual barriers and learned to accept that there are supernatural events in our lives, we see there is something in these moments that belies chance. They are more than just beneficially timed coincidences. For those who have experienced them, there is an absolute awareness of the incredible message they represent. We sense their significance, not as something to be worshipped in itself, but as a *gift* from one worthy of worship. They are a reminder of the loving hand of God on the heavily burdened shoulder, one that helps wipe away the seemingly endless tears while soothing the anguish in our souls. They are seen not only with our physical eyes but with our spiritual eyes as well. They are natural things—not visions or apparitions—linked together by God in space and time in a meaningful, revealing way.

The true value in these "little miracles" lies in how we who perceive them ultimately and use them. If we turn them into objects of worship, then they are misused. They become "false gods" despite their true purpose, and we undermine and destroy their intended value. If we chase after them, we are moving in the wrong direction. They are a gift to us. We do not and cannot make them happen. In and of themselves, they are unimportant.

But if we praise the loving God who provides them, making Him the object of our worship, then they can more fully serve His purpose and feed our spiritual growth.

I am personally convinced that these events represent a sort of tap on the shoulder from God. We often become more aware of these indications of God's presence in our lives when we are seeking Him most diligently. At these times of great need we finally turn away from our limited strength to discover that if we seek, we will find; if we knock, the door will be opened; if we ask, we will receive.

As we bound through the highs and wade through the lows of earthly life, God is always there—it is we who place the distance between us and Him. We are the ones who may be unaware of God's presence due to our own preoccupation with success and failure or some other distraction in our self-oriented world.

Perhaps in this day of such frequent and dramatic scientific discovery we expect God's presence to manifest itself in some attention-grabbing form. But God's revelations don't always have to come in burning bushes; they may come to us through something as simple as sparrows or foxes at our windows— especially during those highly sensitive moments following unfathomable human loss.

Ironically, despite my increasing awareness of God's presence in my life, I found my path of discovery was not always straight. I was like the canoeist who sets his sights on a point on the distant shore only to paddle a frustrating, zigzagging course as the elements of wind, water, and errant paddle strokes work against him. He may occasionally even lose sight of his goal as mists rise up between him and his destination, obscuring the shoreline he is moving toward. But if he persists, he will find his way again and the landfall, once attained, will be all the more meaningful.

On my journey I turned many corners that led only to blind alleyways—alleyways always devoid of light. Even though I was now searching diligently for God's presence in my life, my desire was for Him to conform to my image. The God I was seeking was one who required nothing more of man than generic recognition, a God who could be reached by a variety of comfortable human pathways.

Fortunately God gave me the time I needed to find my way through the many diversions I explored. Moving from books

on reincarnation and psychic phenomenon to Christian literature, one thing became clear to me: the books on psychic
phenomena, reincarnation, and the like were merely an accu-
mulation of speculative material by men who—like me—were
documenting their own opinions on the subjects. Their approach was academic, intellectual, humanistic, and, for me,
ultimately unfulfilling. The theories changed with each new
author I read. The Christian material was different. It all went
back to a single source—the Bible.

One of the most important encouragements for me at the
early stages of seeking was the consistent yet gentle prodding
I received from Christian friends to read the Bible. Regardless
of what advice they gave me, their closing comment always
seemed to be "and read your Bible." At first I saw this encouragement as something trite that Christians say to those who
are on the fence or to those who are on the other side. It seemed
too pat an answer, too easy. "Read your Bible and you'll be
fine." Right.

But I *did* begin to read it, and unlike other works in which
I found little satisfaction for my needs, the Bible awakened
something in me. As I earnestly read God's word, a growing
hunger for truth kindled in my bruised and weary soul for the
first time in my adult life. Along with this hunger came an
ever-increasing spark of hope fed by scripture. I often lay
awake, thinking of the reality of Christ's sacrifice on the
cross—not as an abstract historical event, but on a very personal level, for me. I thought of the parallel between my pain
due to Christopher's death and God's own pain as His only
Son died on the cross. Jesus' suffering and death became
very personal to me, and I realized I had put Him there as
surely as the Scribes, Pharisees, and Romans had done almost two thousand years before. As I accepted all that Jesus'
life, death, and resurrection meant for me, I began to be
filled with the peace promised in the Bible—the peace that
"passes all understanding"—because through Jesus' death
and resurrection I found a hope that transcended the limits
and suffering of earthly life. The hope is for eternal life, un-
marred by suffering and tears, eternal life spent in the pres-

ence of the God of all creation, eternal life with Christopher and others I love.

I suppose the most remarkable aspect of the growing peace I have found is the way it has gently softened Christopher's loss. The void left by his death continues to be filled with the recognition of Christ's love for me and my deepening love for Him. It goes a long way towards easing my pain and destroying my fear of my own death.

Please don't misunderstand me; Christopher's death remains the most significant and painful event of my life. But God's grace has been sufficient to ease even that immense pain—for I have found Him more powerful than death. Jesus' victory over the grave has left us with an opportunity for peace and hope—the hope for a similar resurrection.

Yet even as I came close to attaining this hope I found myself asking some very difficult questions about the nature of God. One question in particular seemed to plague me: Why would a loving God allow so much pain in the lives of those He loves?

As sure as ever God puts his children in the furnace,
He will be in the furnace with them.
C. H. Spurgeon, *Privileges of Trial*

CHAPTER 16

A Loving God?

My personal awakening to the possibilities of faith was inspired by the depth of my pain. I doubt that anything less devastating could have captured such undivided attention from me. While I do not hold God responsible for the pain I felt, I am confident now that such times are used to draw us closer. You see, in my despair I began desperately looking for hope only to find that it seemed that there could be no hope without faith. Where faith exists, or where it can be nurtured and begins to grow, God reaches out to us and raises us away from the pain and chaos of our deepest troubles. While God does not promise us immunity from these troubles, He does promise relief for those who turn to Him.

Pain knows no strangers. It is a part of everyone's life. Understanding why a loving God would allow such agony is one of the most difficult considerations we face. For many who would believe in God, pain and suffering are the primary obstacles to the growth of their belief. For others who are certain that there is no God, pain is just another undesirable, unpleasant part of living. Its presence is grudgingly accepted as an unpredictable element of fate in a world of chance. But for those who place their faith and trust in God, a more meaningful answer to the problem of pain, as well as to its purpose, must be sought.

Let's start by considering the most familiar type of pain: physical pain. What value does this discomfort serve? The answer is surprising: physical pain, as unpleasant as it may be, ultimately protects us from more serious injury. This form of pain mobilizes our bodies to move away from things that would hurt or even destroy us. It causes us to withdraw our fingers from the hot stove top; without feeling pain we might leave them there and be severely burned. The reflex saves us from more serious injury. Mercifully when an injury exceeds the limits of pain our bodies can tolerate, we usually lose consciousness or a physical numbness relieves our suffering.

Emotional pain works in much the same way but on a far deeper level. Small emotional hurts generate equally small reflexive withdrawals from the source of the pain. A friend gossips about us; we learn of the gossip and take a step back from the friendship for a while. Later we can reestablish contact and work out our misunderstandings. Devastating emotional pain—caused by the death of a child, for example—has a far greater impact. It often numbs us in much the same way as a severe physical injury causes numbness. It can affect us so much that we might lose consciousness—either literally or figuratively—as we seek somehow to escape its unpleasant presence.

The important thing to understand about pain is that through its presence in our lives we are brought to focus not only on the pain itself but on its source and our relationship to the source. Physical pain teaches us to be more cautious about sources of physical danger, while emotional pain warns us to look at dangers of the psyche—to look at who we are, where we are, where we are headed.

So this, in a simplified sense, is the basic purpose of pain. But for those who believe in God difficult questions remain: Why does God allow *extreme* pain, either emotional or physical, to enter into our lives? Is He using it to teach us a lesson?

Is this God's idea of instruction? He is a loving God, isn't He? In His omniscience, isn't there some other less devastating way to accomplish the same purpose?

Most of us see a loving God as one who would protect us from all pain, from hurt, and from suffering—a sort of God of "good times." But we must ask ourselves, "In our pain-free moments, do we draw near to God and grow spiritually, or do we lose ourselves in our pleasure and self-indulgence?" Isn't it during the most severe encounters with pain and suffering—during the "hard times"—that we most often learn the true meaning of love and the most profound lessons? Isn't it then that we see most clearly the deeper things of this life? When the tornado rips its way through a sleeping town, when an earthquake strikes a distant Russian village, when we see emaciated children on some Ethiopian plain, isn't that when we are truly touched and when we are moved to try to help those less fortunate? And when personal tragedy is part of our own lives it evokes even deeper responses. Could it be, perhaps, that God is at work in our pain, using it somehow for a greater purpose? A purpose that may be beyond our ability to comprehend?

I was particularly affected by the death of a coworker named Maureen. Her story is a classic study of pain as a teacher. A beautiful and gracious lady, Maureen fought an almost superhuman battle with cancer. It first appeared many years earlier, and, over time, had relentlessly torn away at her body. Yet during the entire course of her illness I never heard her complain.

When my cancer was discovered, Maureen was the first person I went to. We were able to share a light moment as we discussed our illness. "Well, I guess now we are members of the same club," I told her. She smiled at me, and said, "Yes, but remember, I'm still the president. You'll have to settle for vice president, because I'm not going anywhere for a long time and neither are you."

Maureen's courageous battle with cancer and her upbeat attitude reflected her faith in a radiant way. As a friend and I were discussing Maureen's patient, uncomplaining way of cop-

ing with her illness one day, the friend raised an understand-
able question. "I just can't fathom how a loving God could
allow Maureen to suffer like this. She is such a good person; it
just isn't fair."

"But if Maureen weren't such a good person, how would
you feel about her illness and suffering?" I asked. "Of
course you'd never wish an illness like this on anyone, but if
they weren't such a good person, you and I could probably
rationalize that somehow they deserved it. Seeing someone
like Maureen go through this without complaining, with so
much patience and love, is a far better statement of God's
grace than would be the person who we feel 'deserves it.'
Maybe that's why God has chosen her—to teach us about His
loving grace."

Maureen and her acceptance of pain reminds me of a simple
story from the Bible, one in which Jesus healed a blind man
near the pool of Siloam. "As he went along, he saw a man
blind from birth. His disciples asked him, 'Rabbi, who sinned,
this man or his parents, that he was born blind?' 'Neither this
man nor his parents sinned,' said Jesus, 'but this happened so
that the work of God might be displayed in his life" (John
9:1–3). When we look at pain in this light, we begin to see it
differently.

But even if we are successful in reaching the point of accepting the presence of most of the pain in our own lives, how
do we reconcile our feelings about the tremendous hurt resulting from the death of our child? The death of a child is absolutely contrary to all we expect in life because we, the parents,
were supposed to depart first. It devastates us and leaves us
broken. Surely no loving God would allow this to happen.

Even those who learn to trust God in the face of life's most
severe tests will likely continue to search for answers for this
particular type of tragedy. As we search, we may move closer
to resolution if we rethink how we view the framework within
which these tragedies occur; or, more specifically, how we
view life itself.

Our natural tendency is to weigh life's events against our time on earth—a limited perspective indeed. In doing so, death becomes the ultimate tragedy—an enemy we try to defeat via doctors, medications, and "life support" systems. Yet if we step back from this narrow vantage point and see life as comprising both this limited earthly segment and an eternal portion yet to come, death is much less of an enemy. Instead, it becomes a point of transition, one that takes us from this world into the next.

As I began to look at life as being eternal, I was better able to approach an understanding of what God's perspective might be. His view of human life includes its physical entirety—from beginning to end—as well as the incomprehensible portion that lies beyond mortality. From this omniscient vantage point, the death of a child and our other worldly sufferings must serve an essential purpose in God's plan for each of us.

We can reasonably argue that the actual event of death and the sorrow it leaves behind surely cannot be beneficial. But if any of us fully understood the way each life event is used, we would have no need for God, for we would be as wise as He. We do not understand fully because we are not omniscient. In our humanness, we may benefit by considering a very intriguing biblical promise: "All things work together for good to them that love God." (Romans 8:28)

God and only God knows how the pieces of the puzzle fit together, how they work toward an ultimate good. He alone has an eternal perspective, unlimited by the boundaries of time that constrain us humans. For us the issue must not be having the answer to every question; it must be learning to trust—even when there are no easy answers.

Reflect again for a moment on Romans 8:28. Focus on the word "together." God's message does not say that each individual event will in itself be good, but that it will work *together* with the other events in our lives for good if we love Him. Through God's plan, we learn invaluable lessons from all of life's events—both the good and the bad. While the devastation of losing a child may seem impossible to reconcile with the idea that it may somehow work for good, we must once again remember how limited our earthly perspective is.

We see the tragic event initially from the viewpoint of our pain alone, but as time broadens our perspective we may see "good" coming from our hurt. We find we may experience new levels of spiritual maturity that allow us to reach out in true love to others who are in pain. We may find that lives around us are affected dramatically by our loss. Other parents have told us countless times how Christopher's death had changed their own attitudes and actions toward their children—for the better.

Despite the good that may occur, the scale may still seem disturbingly off balance. There is no doubt that the death of a child is the supreme test of our love for God. It is a leap of faith to be able to trust God completely in every event in our lives—and especially in this one.

Even should we reach this level of trust, the pain of separation from those we love will remain. But we may find a more peaceful acceptance of the loss of the life of our loved one in knowing that their life is not over, only transformed. Like a friend who has gone ahead of us in a journey, they wait for us at a place beyond our view. As we come closer to this point of understanding, we see that those who have departed this life have attained the ultimate goal: to be with God.

Not all are able to respond to death this way. Some are unable to rise above the despair even after prolonged grieving. They find themselves locked into a period of extended withdrawal from life and from any relationship with God. They struggle alone although surrounded by people who would help them if they could. They operate in a world devoid of hope.

I am not suggesting that any parent should fail to grieve over the loss of a child or other loved ones. (Remember, even Jesus wept at the death of his friend Lazarus.) I am saying that those who place their trust in God need not grieve as those who have no hope. As Paul wrote to the Thessalonians, "Brothers we do not want you to be ignorant about those who fall asleep (die), or to grieve like the rest of men, who have no hope. We believe that Jesus died and rose again and so we believe that God will

bring with Jesus those who have fallen asleep in Him.''
(1Thessalonians 4:13–14 NIV).

In the grief that comes from the separation brought about by
death, we can find solace in the promise of an eternal reunion
with those we love. From this perspective, our pain is bearable,
our broken lives can heal, and our loss is not without hope.

Hope is like the sun, which, as we journey towards it, casts the shadow of our burden behind us.
SAMUEL SMILES, *Self-Help*

CHAPTER 17 ·

Hope

"HOPE SPRINGS ETERNAL." A familiar quote. My own experience connects hope and the eternal in a different way. For me, it is the very idea that life is eternal that is the basis for my hope.

When I am able to view life from an eternal perspective, the day-to-day problems lose their grip on me. It is not that they are no longer important or unnecessary to resolve but that their relationship to the ultimate outcome of my experience is less critical, less threatening. I am able to view them with less anxiety, with an eye focussed on the bigger picture.

Christopher's death played an ironic role in my life. More than anything else that has ever happened to me, it could have completely destroyed any element of hope in my life. But as I sought a deeper understanding of life, sought the truth about God and His mysteries, my spirit began to pull away from the immobilizing grip of my loss. Set against the background of my unfathomable pain, the spark of hope kindled and grew into a consuming flame. Hope illuminated my being, filled me with new light—light far more powerful than the heavy darkness that had engulfed me as the result of the tragedy in my life.

One of the foundations for my growing hope was an acceptance of the idea that God truly has a plan for our lives. In contrast to this was the philosophy set forth in *When Bad Things Happen to Good People* by Rabbi Harold Kushner. While some of his insights were helpful, Rabbi Kushner painted the picture of a God not in control—a God without a plan. This God stands by helplessly, watching the chaos of creation, which has turned into something like a runaway nuclear reactor. Started at the beginning of time, God's out-of-control work assaults us with natural disasters, accidents, and other tragedies from which He is unable to protect us. Through mere chance we are bombarded with an endless assault of painful events that cease only when we die. This sort of God would be no better than a mad scientist who unleashes mayhem from his laboratory then steps back and watches as it destroys the world. Who could worship such a God? Who could find hope in a relationship with a God like this?

I instead find my hope in a God who is in control. He has compensated for evil in the world through resurrection. He is a God of eternal life, a God who defeated death itself. If we hold these beliefs, where does this hope take us? In my case, the resulting spiritual awakening peacefully put to rest the fear of my own death and the emptiness over Christopher's death as well. This dramatic experience was not some convenient escape plan that I conjured up to elude my pain. I assure you my strength alone is far too limited to succeed at such an effort. The peace I have found has come from outside my limited human resources. It has come through God's grace.

Reaching this point of peace was not easy. There were choices to be made along the way. Instead of "knocking" on the spiritual door when I did, I could have kept the door closed, locking out the peace that waited on the other side. Some people choose to do just that as they allow questions that cannot be answered to stand in the way of true spirituality and the peace that accompanies it. They cling to the limits of what they *know*, regardless of how it may limit them.

Letting go of intellectual solutions and other substitutes for genuine spirituality is frightening because for many of us they are the basis of our very reality, even our practice of faith. We have grown up with the textbook and with sometimes limiting traditions. Both were made by man and both may stand as formidable barriers to our spiritual growth. To give them up means to admit we have been shortsighted in the past. To give them up means we step out of the boat and onto the stormy seas—alone perhaps—just as the Apostle Peter did some two thousand years ago. Yet if we fail to do so, we may lock ourselves within these man-made and self-imposed boundaries, denying ourselves the true peace that lies beyond.

My advice to those of you who struggle with spiritually limiting issues like these is to ask the world of science and intellect to give you answers that work for your pain and to show you how to fill the emptiness inside you. When these answers have failed, as I am certain they will, ask yourself if you want to live the rest of your lifetime without hope simply because you have chosen not to trust in God. I realize that if you have no faith, my candor on this issue may seem rather black and white, but please remember, I have stood where you now stand. I, too, stood rather poorly equipped at the time. These were the same issues that I had to face. And I cannot imagine any parent—atheist, agnostic, Buddhist, Jewish, Hindu, Muslim, Christian—who has lost a child, who will not face head-on the ultimate mystery of death and in doing so also confront the existence of God and man's relationship to Him.

In her book *The Bereaved Parent*, Harriet Sarnoff Schiff offers a quote from a second-generation atheist—a father whose daughter had died—that speaks about his perspective as a nonbeliever. "I look with envy upon those of you who believe. My intellect does not give me this freedom. Since Betty died I have learned that there is little to comfort me in this life. For a nonbeliever faced with the death of his child there are not too many places to turn."

If you ask yourself, as I did, who God is, remember that in all of history there have been only a handful of religious figures whose teachings have survived the critical scrutiny of the world—and of those, only one who claimed to be God. Only one whose coming was prophesied over thousands of years and documented in a book that has survived until today. Only one who claimed to be "the Way, the Truth, and the Life." But most importantly, perhaps, only one who has left an empty tomb. That one is Jesus Christ.

Since losing Christopher I have met many others who have suffered similar losses. Some are still searching after many years for a way to accept what has happened in their lives. They attend seminars, read books, and pursue various other worldly alternatives for coping with their loss only to find that each one leaves them with the same emptiness. But of those who have given their grief over to God, many have found peace and acceptance.

Reaching the point of acceptance where we can give our grief over to God is not easy, nor does it come quickly when tragedy assaults us. It can be a difficult journey, taking months or even years. Those who work through the anger and discover God's love, however, will find positive changes in their lives. Through their experience the lives of those around them may also change in positive ways as well. Those who learn to trust in God will find their love for others deepening, and at some point they may even begin to see the perfection of God's plan despite the pain.

As you try to sort it all out, think about a tapestry that when viewed from the back side appears as a tangled web of threads and loose ends with no pattern or order. Yet when you step to the other side—and someday each of us will step to the other side—you see the skillful way in which the weaver has brought the individual threads together to create a masterful work—a work not even hinted at on the backside. The Bible offers a beautifully worded parallel to this analogy. "For now we see through a glass, darkly; but then face to face; now I know in part; but then shall I know even as I am known" (1 Corinthians 13:12).

For believers God's word is an unaltering promise—a promise of eternal life. With the same free will we so often misuse, each of us has the choice of trusting this remarkable promise. The choice is ours and ours alone. While the tests God allows in our lives are often severe, I have found, as have countless others, that the power of this promise and God's grace is sufficient—even in the loss of a child.

I mentioned earlier that the minister at the service in our hometown read a poem entitled "God's Lent Child." The poem was sent to President Calvin Coolidge many years ago after the death of his son. For those of us who have lost children the words ring especially true.

> I'll lend you for a little time
> A child of mine, God said.
> For you to love the while he lives
> And mourn for when he's dead.
>
> It may be six or seven years
> Or twenty-two or three.
> But will you, till I call him back,
> Take care of him for me?
>
> He'll bring his charms to gladden you
> And shall his stay be brief,
> You'll have his lovely memories
> As solace for your grief.
>
> I cannot promise he will stay
> Since all from earth return,
> But there are lessons taught down there
> I want this child to learn.
>
> I've looked the wide world over
> In my search for teachers true.
> And from the throngs that crowd life's lane
> I have selected you.
>
> Now will you give him all your love,
> Nor think the labor vain,
> Nor hate me when I come to call
> To take him back again.

I fancied that I heard them say,
"Dear Lord, thy will be done.
For all the joy thy child shall bring,
The risk of grief we'll run.

"We'll shelter him with tenderness.
We'll love him while we may,
And for the happiness we've known.
Forever grateful stay.

"But shall the angels call for him
Much sooner than we've planned,
We'll brave the bitter grief that comes
And try to understand."

My family and I have sought to understand. If you have lost a child, you have tried to do the same. While we miss Christopher immensely, his short life and his death have intensified the element of love in our lives—for Christopher, for each other, for those around us, *and* for God. Perhaps this is the lesson, albeit painful to undergo, that God would have us learn from all the tragedies that befall us: that love is the essence of this life and that any experience that truly deepens it is serving a greater good.

The Bible speaks especially clearly on this point. "Let us love one another, for love comes from God. Everyone who loves has been born of God and knows God. Whoever does not love does not know God, because *God is love*" (1 John 4:7–8).

When we named Christopher, I had no particular interest in the meaning of his name. Only after his death did I learn that it is derived from the same Greek in which the original text of the New Testament was written. Christopher's name means "Christ bearer."

As I look back with a grateful heart for the time we had together with Christopher, I see that his short life did that just; it has brought me Christ in a way I had never experienced before. And it also allows me to look ahead with hope to a time of eternal reunion in God's presence where there will be no more mourning or tears, no more pain . . . and no more death.

About the Author

JOHN BRAMBLETT attended the United States Naval Academy at Annapolis and holds a master's degree in environmental science from the Johns Hopkins University in Baltimore. In addition to his job as a management analyst, he works as a volunteer at a local pediatric hospital and at a camp for children with cancer. He lives in Vermont with his wife, Mairi, and three children: John, Brian, and Meghan.